A rain squall was sweeping in on the island, and the Jap bombers came in behind it, hidden from view until they were on top of us. Nobody heard them. The surf on the reefs around the island made it hard to hear motors, but even so the Japs took no chances. They cut off their motors and came down on us in a silent glide behind the mask of the squall.

It was 11:50 a.m.

At the Pan-American Hotel, the Clipper passengers were lunching and wondering how badly Pearl Harbor had been hit.

I was on the telephone in my office. I was giving some routine instructions to Lieutenant Wally Lewis at Peacock Point when he suddenly broke in: "Major, there's a squadron of planes coming in from the south. Are they friendly?"

It was 11:58.

The gliding bombers were almost on top of us when they broke out of the rain squall at barely two thousand feet. A civilian yelled, "Look! Their wheels are falling off!" Only it wasn't wheels. Over the phone, Lewis was yelling, "They're dropping bombs!"

The next instant, I heard the first bombs exploding.

This is the ultimate book on Wake Island, written by the man who directed its defense. James P.S. Devereux provides an enormously exciting and important eyewitness account of how an undermanned and outgunned garrison courageously defended their tiny Pacific outpost for sixteen days—at a time when America was perilously close to disaster!

WAKE
ISLAND

JAMES P.S. DEVEREUX
Brigadier General, USMC (Ret.)

MAJOR BOOKS • CANOGA PARK, CALIFORNIA

Originally published as *The Story of Wake Island* by J.B. Lippincott Company, Philadelphia & New York

Revised and Enlarged Edition
Copyright © 1978 by James P.S. Devereux
All rights reserved

MAJOR BOOKS
21335 Roscoe Boulevard
Canoga Park, California 91304

Printed in the United States of America

ISBN 0-89041-208-1

Library of Congress Catalog
Card Number: 78-63624

TO THE MEN WHO SERVED IN THE DEFENSE

OF WAKE ISLAND

ARMY, NAVY, MARINES AND CIVILIANS

AUTHOR'S NOTE

This account of the defense of Wake Island was originally written without benefit of notes and records, which were destroyed by the Japanese or by us to prevent capture. This account is as accurate as the author could make it from his own recollection, available records and the recollection of other Wake Island veterans, both officers and men. Additional and corrective data has been added for this 1978 edition from official publications, especially The Defense of Wake *by R.D. Heinl. Nevertheless, the Department of the Navy is in no way responsible for any points of view expressed nor for the factual accuracy of statements made.*

CONTENTS

Preface

by

Robert E. Sherwood

[Note: Robert E. Sherwood's comments were written for the first edition of this book at a time when James P.S. Devereux held the military rank of colonel. Although more than three decades old, the original Preface has been retained for this new edition because Mr. Sherwood's words, once currently significant, are now historically significant, and provide a perceptive lead-in to a most remarkable episode in American military history.]

THIS BOOK IS WRITTEN BY an American fighting man. It makes no pretensions to literary style or significance. It is not based on hearsay or latrine gossip. It reveals no secrets as to what really went on "at the highest levels"—indeed, Colonel Devereux makes it entirely clear that he never had the faintest idea of what was happening at the highest levels.

All he knew was that he was in command of the garrison on Wake Island when war broke out in the Pacific, and that he was to hold this island for as long as was humanly possible. He did so.

His story of this memorable fight is enormously exciting and stimulating and important.

In the first two weeks of American participation in the Second World War, many people were extremely uncertain of our ability to fight against the known and (up to then) all-conquering power of the Nazis and the surprising power suddenly revealed by the Japanese.

It had been a long time since any American forces had been compelled to raise the white flag of surrender, and the big question was: could we take it? The British had proved that they could take it; so had the Russians and the Chinese. But—our enemies were saying that we were so gorged with success that we had become soft and flabby and complacent and there were some among our own people who feared that this was true.

Two days after Pearl Harbor, President Franklin D. Roosevelt said, over the radio, "The reports from Guam and Wake and Midway are still confused, but we must be prepared for the announcement that all these three outposts have been seized."

Defenseless Guam was doomed because the Congress had been unable to understand that an island eight thousand miles from Washington could be of vital importance to the security of the Western Hemisphere, so the Japanese took it and it eventually cost us greatly to take it back.

At Midway, the enemy chose not to attack until, in early June, 1942, he felt ready to move on to much greater prizes.

The Japanese attacked little Wake the day of Pearl Harbor, first with devastating bombing and subsequently with substantial naval and ground forces. Immediately, this obscure atoll became a symbol of national tragedy and individual glory. The pathetically small garrison, by holding out for fourteen historic days, and inflicting tremendous losses on the enemy, gave to the American spirit the kick that it needed. Our people gained the will to fight and the confidence in our ability to fight, and this was done, literally, "with the help of God and a few Marines."

What was important about the garrison of Wake— and Colonel Devereux emphasizes this in this book—is that they were not exceptional, they were no supermen from the "comic" strips. Had they not been on Wake another outfit would have been there and Colonel Devereux is certain that it would have behaved in much the same creditable manner as his own. But it was Devereux's detachment which was there and the officers and men of that shockingly ill-equipped outfit proved to their countrymen and to the whole world that Americans of 1941 could take it and could also dish it out.

As long as I live, I can never forget the emotional upheaval that I experienced when I looked at the front page of the *New York Times* on the morning of December 25, 1941. The remnants of the garrison had surrendered. There was a photograph of Major (as he was then) Devereux—a thin, sensitive face, very unlike the rugged *What Price Glory?* Marine as impersonated by Louis Wolheim or Victor McLaglen.

Over this photograph the *Times* printed two great words: *Semper Fidelis*—the motto of the United States Marine Corps to which the men of Wake had been so conspicuously faithful.

A little over three years later (February 15, 1945) I had the privilege and pleasure of being on board an aircraft carrier approaching Tokyo. It was *USS Bennington* (CV-20), a unit of the powerful fleet known as Task Force 58. This was the first time in the war that the U.S. Navy reached the Japanese home islands and struck.

I was in the Ready Room of a group of USMC flyers who used F4U fighter planes (Corsairs). This group was being briefed on their forthcoming mission— the first they knew that the target was Tokyo. Only a few of them had ever been in combat before. All of them looked excited and many of them looked scared.

The officer conducting the briefing talked in the usual cold, impersonal manner of the problems involved. But when the routine was completed, the speaker became less impersonal.

He said, "There are some prisoner-of-war camps in this target area. In these camps are members of the Marine Corps, including undoubtedly some of the survivors of the garrison of Wake Island. They have been prisoners of the Japs for more than three years. When these men look up and see us we must be sure to be flying at a low enough altitude so that they will know who we are."

The reinforcements which never came to the men on Wake were now coming to them on the Japanese homeland itself. They were coming in a fleet more powerful than all of the prewar navies of the world put together.

Our Navy by then was ranging all over the Western Pacific, our Air Forces were in the skies over East Asia and Europe, our ground forces were fighting in Burma and northern Italy and on the Rhine. The production of arms was gigantic beyond belief. And the scientists, in Oak Ridge and Los Alamos, were coming to the end of their long, secret labors to perfect the weapon of ultimate extinction.

In the realization of the overwhelming power which was finally achieved, we must forever remember that no part of it would have been possible had it not been for the demonstrations of basic guts that were given us in the beginning at Dunkirk and Leningrad and Wake Island.

Colonel Devereux served his country well then. He has served it well again by writing this book. He reminds us how perilously close we were to disaster. He reminds us that no matter how large or rich or proud a nation may be, it cannot win a war if it lacks the essential quality of courage—and that goes also for the winning of a peace.

The White House
Washington
5 January 1942

Citation by

THE PRESIDENT OF THE UNITED STATES

of

The Wake detachment of the 1st Defense Battalion, U.S. Marine Corps, under command of Major James P.S. Devereux, U.S. Marines

and

Marine Fighting Squadron 211 of Marine Aircraft Group 21, under command of Major Paul A. Putnam, U.S. Marines

The courageous conduct of the officers and men of these units, who defended Wake Island against an overwhelming superiority of enemy air, sea, and land attacks from December 8 to 22, 1941, has been noted with admiration by their fellow countrymen and the civilized world, and will not be forgotten so long as gallantry and heroism are respected and honored. These units are commended for their devotion to duty and splendid conduct at their battle stations under the most adverse conditions. With limited defensive means against attacks in great force, they manned their shore installations and flew their aircraft so well that five enemy warships were either sunk or severely damaged, many hostile planes shot down, and an unknown number of land troops destroyed.

Author's Introduction

During the days of 1940 and early 1941, there were few officers of any of our armed services who were not convinced that the United States would inevitably be drawn into the war already raging in Europe and to a lesser extent in Asia. The conflict would thus become truly global in scope. Most certainly our national interests in both Europe and Asia were deeply involved in the issues at stake and it seemed impossible to cling to peace over the long haul or possibly even over the short haul. Few of us realized how close our war actually was; nonetheless, we were sure that it was coming.

Accordingly, a great many measures had been taken by our military authorities to put our nation on a war footing. Reserve forces had been called to active duty, the draft had been legislated into effect, and the intensity of training programs had been considerably stepped up. Large-scale maneuvers had been conducted by all services; from them, lessons had been learned and much valuable training had been given. Industry was well along the road to mobilization and was producing much needed new equipment at a significant rate. The redesign and evaluation of our old, and in many cases obsolete, equipment was in progress; the organizational structure of military units at all levels was being studied intensely, and lessons learned from maneuvers and from observation of the European war were being incorporated into a thorough overhaul.

When the Japanese actually struck on December 7th (8th Wake time), our armed forces were about half way along the road toward readiness for combat. All services were short of men, critically short of equipment, and also much training still had to be done. In the realization that our entry into the war was imminent, our higher commanders deployed understrength units armed with inadequate, and in some cases obsolescent, equipment to what were believed to be the most vital points of our national defense. When war came, this policy bought time in that it forced the Japanese to pay in manpower, equipment, and time for the gains they made. It did, however, spell almost certain defeat for the forces deployed.

It fell to my lot, more or less by chance as the text describes, to be the coordinator of the Wake Island defense force when war was imminent. I did not dwell much upon the matter at the time, but I fully realized that from the very beginning of war we would almost certainly be a prime target for attack. The importance of Wake as a military outpost in the Western Pacific was no secret. That the Japs recognized it as well as we did is well demonstrated by the size of the effort mounted to seize the island at the outset of hostilities. Even so, the defense situation on Wake reflected quite accurately the state of our national preparation for war as of late 1941.

The island was garrisoned by a detachment of the 1st Marine Defense Battalion and by a Marine Fighter Squadron, VMF 211. Both of these units were short of many vital items of equipment, as I shall describe in some detail. My officers and noncommissioned officers were experienced and trained, but I also had recruits of no more than four months' service. The force was over fifty percent short of authorized personnel, and even with our inadequate supply of equipment we did not have enough troops to man all of our weapons.

The deficiencies, or at least the most obvious ones, were recognized by higher authority and without doubt would have been corrected in due course on a piecemeal basis. Had war been delayed by, let us say a year, we would have very probably been reinforced, properly equipped, and would have had time to develop our defenses. Under such conditions we would have had an excellent chance to defend Wake successfully against anything the enemy could throw at us. The enemy permitted us no such a luxury.

The principal lesson to be learned from the experience of Wake Island, which I describe in this book, is that if a commander is assigned a mission he must be given the means to accomplish it, otherwise he is doomed to defeat.

In the total context of World War II, the Wake Island operation was minute. I believe, however, that it was important to the national war effort out of proportion to its size. In the first place, we were able to delay for two important weeks the powerful thrust of the Japanese initial attack. We tied up a significant amount of naval strength for a brief interval, which allowed the battered forces at Pearl Harbor to reorganize. This broke the momentum and timing of the Japanese offensive.

Of more importance to the nation as a whole, however, Wake was a symbol. The surprise and defeat at Pearl Harbor left almost everyone in the country shocked and confused; all eyes sought desperately for scraps of evidence that we were still alive and in the fight. Wake Island and several other similar battles showed all confused United States citizens that while we might not yet be ready for total war, "Our hearts were in the trim," to use the words of Shakespeare's King

Henry V. We thus provided a slender but necessary base of pride and confidence to which everyone could rally and unite with the assurance that all was not lost—that we could and would face up to the war which had been thrust upon us and win it.

I am proud, as I believe all of my fellow Wake Island Marines are, to have been a part of that defense. I would like, however, to point out most emphatically that there was nothing special about any one of us who chanced to be on Wake when war broke. We were simply average Marines manning a defense point because we had been placed there by competent authority and had been ordered to defend it. This order, when the moment arrived, we carried out to the best of our professional ability in the tradition of the Marine Corps, not because it might gain us publicity or fame, but simply because it was our duty to do so. No man on Wake sought glory or glamour. Such ideas never entered our heads, mainly, I suppose, because we were too busy, but more importantly because we were Marines doing what was expected of us. How well we succeeded in doing our duty in this action must be decided by each reader as he goes through this book.

The fight for Wake Island will, I hope, be preserved in memory as a bright mark in the illustrious history of the American Armed Forces. It should serve as further proof, though none is really needed, that the most effective piece of combat equipment yet designed by mankind is the American fighting man. Major Paul Putnam's final report said most truthfully, "All hands have behaved splendidly and held up in a manner of which the Marine Corps may well tell."

This book is about Marines and an episode in the existence of a Marine Corps unit. Most of the praise for duty well done is given to Marines, but I do not mean by this to overlook the outstanding work of the officers and men of the Army and Navy who were on Wake Island. To a man this small group rallied to the cause and fitted themselves into our defense effort most effectively.

When war came there were about one thousand civilians on Wake Island, mostly engineers and workmen under contract with the Navy for the construction of the airfield and living accommodations. It was planned to evacuate most of these men aboard the ships of Task Force 14 which sailed from Pearl Harbor on December 15th to relieve us. The relief was diverted in midpassage, so all of the civilians were with us to the end.

Many of these men, though they were under no obligation to do so, served valiantly alongside our military personnel. They carried ammunition to the guns, they served as cannoniers, and in some cases they fought as infantrymen in the ranks. The work done by the small civilian medical group was particularly worthy of praise. When the end came, the civilians were taken prisoners along with the rest of us and were hauled off to spend the war in prison camps. I must say that they showed themselves to be loyal and patriotic Americans.

James P.S. Devereux
September, 1978

Chapter One

Mission To Wake

WAKE ISLAND IS A SPIT-KIT of sand and coral without any reason for being except the birds and rats which were its only native inhabitants. Then an accident of geography made it a military blue chip. The battle of Wake lasted sixteen days and more than five thousand men were killed, but it would never have been fought except for that accident. So you must understand the geography of Wake and you must know a few unpleasant facts if you would understand the battle for the island. I will try to keep this background brief, but I will put it down at the start because I think the story of Wake Island, the full story, should be told at last.

Wake is so small, so remote and so barren that more than a hundred years of its history can be told in three sentences. It was discovered by the British in 1796, visited by the American explorer Charles Wilkes in 1841 and claimed as an American possession in 1899 by Captain E.D. Taussig, USN. It was worthless except as a bird sanctuary. It remained uninhabited until Pan-American Airways established a station there for refueling its trans-Pacific Clippers in 1935.

Japan—and that accident of geography—changed all that. The crisis in the Pacific made Wake a valuable piece of real estate. It ceased to be merely a micro-

scopic atoll of useless coral and scrubby brush. It
became valuable as an outpost on our Sea Frontier, a
link in the chain of widely separated American islands
that stretched from Dutch Harbor in the Aleutians
almost to the Equator. These outposts were our first
line of defense. They were intended to form a screen
against Japan much as blockhouses strung across the
western plains formed a screen against hostile tribes in
the days of our Indian wars.

Pearl Harbor was the core of this frontier defense.
Nearest to Hawaii, guarding its western approaches,
were Midway, Johnston and Palmyra. From Pearl Harbor, Midway was less than twelve hundred miles to the
northwest, Johnston seven hundred miles to the southwest, Palmyra about nine hundred miles to the south.

Far westward, two thousand miles from Pearl Harbor, lay lonely Wake. It was nearer to the mainland of
Japan than to Hawaii. It lay almost on the boundary
line of the Japanese mandate. The powerful Japanese
bases in the Marshalls, almost due south of Wake,
were hardly six hundred miles away. The nearest Jap
base was Taongi, three hundred twenty-five miles to the
south. The nearest American bases were more than
three times as far from Wake—Midway about a
thousand miles to the east, Guam twelve hundred
miles to the west. Of all the American outposts, Wake
was the nearest to Japan and the nearest, except Guam,
to Japanese island bases.

Though its isolation made Wake one of our most
vulnerable outposts, the same geographical factor made
it a more serious potential threat to the Japanese.
Wake lay almost athwart the most direct route between
the Japanese homeland and Tarawa, Jaluit, Kwajalein
and the other Jap bases in the Gilberts and the
Marshalls. If properly developed, and if the Americans
could hold Wake, bombers based there would be able to
strike at Japan's precious bases to the south. Wake
would be able to give land-based air support to any

task force we might send to attack the Pacific area Japan had acquired by mandate after World War I. Patrol planes based on Wake would be able to keep under surveillance—and bombers to attack—hundreds of miles of sea lanes the Japanese Navy regarded as its own.

Our stategists realized the importance of these frontier outposts and pushed a construction program to turn these far-flung island bases into naval air stations, potential springboards for offensive blows as well as defense. The work was being done by civilian contractors under the supervision of Navy engineers. Airfields were being built and shipping facilities created or improved. Barracks, fuel storage tanks, warehouses, all the installations for living and defense were being put in. It was an elaborate program, little Wake alone being a $20,000,000 project. When the program was finished, scouting by long-range patrol planes would make Pearl Harbor, at least theoretically, invulnerable to surprise attack. This patrol network would enable our Navy, at least theoretically, to intercept and engage at a position of our choosing any Jap task force attempting to strike at Hawaii. The only question in 1941 was whether the construction program could be completed before the start of the war we all expected sooner or later.

Wake is really three islands—Wake proper, Wilkes and Peale—forming a roughly U-shaped atoll. If the atoll were a horseshoe, Peacock Point on Wake would be the toe while Wilkes and Peale would be the calks on the ends of the two heels.

Wake proper has an area of less than two square miles; Wilkes and Peale together are considerably less than one square mile in area. The distance from Toki Point on Peale Island to Peacock Point on Wake and back along the other prong of the horseshoe to Kuku Point on Wilkes is only ten miles. The highest point on the island is twenty-one feet above the sea. The larger part of the sand and coral atoll was covered with thick brush and scrub hardwood, a few of the tallest trees being perhaps twenty feet high.

The atoll is entirely surrounded by ragged coral reefs which made it impossible to use the lagoon as a harbor even if it had not been so thickly studded with dangerous coral heads. Ships had to anchor off the southern shore, discharging both passengers and cargo by lightering them to shore. The only entrance to the lagoon even for small craft was the channel between Wake and Wilkes, and that could be used only at high tide. The principal points on the atoll were connected by road, and a bridge joined Wake and Peale, but contact between Wake and Wilkes depended on a small boat ferry.

The island had no natural water supply. The garrison on Wake depended on a sea-water distillation plant and a catchment system which enabled them to store rain water that fell in the short but frequent squalls.

The only wild life on the atoll were the thousands of birds and a strange breed of rats. In addition to the myriad teal, frigate birds, bosun birds, gooneys and all the rest that flocked to the island, there was one weird bird I believe is peculiar to Wake. It was the flightless rail, which looked to me like a tiny cousin of the New Zealand kiwi. I do not know how he ever got to Wake because he can't fly.

The Wake Island rats were no ordinary rodents. They were Polynesian rats—with forelegs very much shorter than their hind legs—and they were the smartest rats I ever expect to see. As Wake was a bird sanctuary, dogs and cats were banned. So the rats flourished. We tried to keep them in check by poison, but they soon learned to ignore the poisoned grain that was scattered for them. They made life miserable for the civilians who set out flower beds around some of the buildings. Even when charged electric wires were strung around the beds, the rats seemed able to figure out ways of getting to the flowers.

When I was ordered from the States to Pearl Harbor early in 1941, I had no reason to suspect that Wake would ever be my personal problem. I was then a major, executive officer in the First Defense Battalion, Lieutenant Colonel Bertram Bone commanding.

At that time, a Marine defense battalion at full training strength consisted of 850 men. Our heaviest weapons were 5-inch guns, the old .51's, formerly used as broadside guns on our battleships. These were for use against surface targets, and we also had batteries of 3-inch antiaircraft guns (AA), as well as machine guns for both AA fire and ground defense.

Though organized primarily as a defense unit, we were more than our name might imply. We were trained in landing operations—in getting guns and heavy gear through the surf—so that we could follow an assault force in a landing and set up artillery defense against air and surface attack. Because of the scarcity of units with such specialized training at that time, the plan was that we should be held back with the striking force while the Army was to garrison the frontier islands.

The plan was changed, however, before we left the States, and we were informed that we would be used for outpost defense. The Navy's district operations officer told me the original plan had been abandoned because "the Army wants the whole place bristling with guns" and the islands were "just too small for all the stuff the Army wants to put on them."

Even then, I still had no reason to think Wake might some day be my worry. The Sixth Defense Battalion was scheduled for Wake while our battalion was to be divided between Johnston and Palmyra. Then it was decided that the Sixth should have more training before being sent to the Sea Frontier. So we were ordered to put a small detachment on Wake until the Sixth should be considered ready to take over. Otherwise, I would not have been on Wake Island.

When I learned at Pearl Harbor that I was to go to Wake as Marine Detachment commander and Island Commander I went to Naval Headquarters and asked that I be briefed on the situation in the area vis-a-vis Japanese forces. I was told in a rather peremptory fashion that this would not be possible because I did not need to know these things.

We garrisoned Wake in August, 1941, and on October fifteenth I arrived there to take command. The garrison consisted of some 180 Marines plus Navy small boat's crews. The Navy had a small group on the island—engineer officers and radio station personnel. There were some twelve hundred civilians on the island. Except for about fifty employees of Pan-American Airways, most of them Chamorros from Guam, the civilians were all employed by the company which had the construction contract.

The Marines were quartered in the old camp which the contractor's men had built for temporary shelter on the west prong of Wake proper when they first reached the island. This was called Camp One. We were housed in tents stretched over frames, with screened sides and wooden decks, and were fairly comfortable. Our living facilities were far less elaborate than those in the civilian camp, but we put up a tent for an Officers' Club and established a PX for the enlisted men. The Marines were permitted to attend the movies at the civilian camp, and there was also swimming and fishing in the lagoon on those rare occasions when the Marines had any free time for recreation.

The contractor's men lived in Camp Two, the new camp built on the east prong of Wake proper. They had a fine setup, with their own hospital, power plant, commissary, refrigeration plant, storehouses, shops and barracks. There were cottages for the civilian executives and the handful of Navy officers. There was also a cottage which we called the White House, not because of any excess of patriotism, but simply because it was white.

The Pan-American Airways station was on Peale Island, with a small modern hotel, its own radio station, shop buildings and a landing dock where the Clipper moored in the lagoon. Two Clippers stopped weekly to refuel, one eastbound and the other westbound, and these arrivals were the Wake Island version of a gala event, especially for any junior officer fortunate enough to be off duty on the infrequent occasions when the passengers included a personable young woman. One balding Britisher became quite upset at the attention shown his pretty blonde secretary, but I never heard that the young lady had any complaint to make.

When I arrived on the island, the contractor's men working on the airfield near the toe of Wake proper had one airstrip in usable condition and were beginning the cross-runway. Five large magazines and three smaller detonator magazines, built of concrete and partly underground, were almost completed in the airfield area. Quarters for the Navy fliers who would be stationed on the island, warehouses and shops also were going up on Wake. On Peale Island, work was progressing on a naval hospital, a Marine barracks, the seaplane ramp and parking area. On Wilkes, there were only fuel storage tanks and the sites of proposed powder magazines, but a new deepwater channel was being cut through the island. In the lagoon, a dredge was removing coral heads from the runways for the seaplanes which were to be based at Wake. Some of these installations were nearly finished; some were partly completed; some were only in the blueprint stage.

As senior line officer on Wake, I was also Island Commander, but the contractor's men were not under my supervision. They were under the contractor's general superintendent, Dan Teters, and the job was being supervised by Lieutenant Commander E.B.

Greey, the Navy engineer. They would come under my orders only in the event of an emergency. Consequently, I could not put civilian crews to work on gun emplacements or other necessary defense installations. The construction program took priority on Wake, and so I had to use my small detachment of Marines to put in our defense installations as best we could. It was mostly pick-and-shovel labor except when the contractor happened to have an idle bulldozer he could lend us for a time.

Both Commander Greey and Mr. Teters gave as much help as they could without taking men and machines from their project. The Marines on Wake were a bit short of equipment and supplies, and I remember that even before the war began we were able to keep our motor transport in full operation only because Mr. Teters gave us spare truck parts from his supply. When we lacked canvas to cover the frames on the Marines' tents, Commander Greey supplied us from the construction project stores. The civilians were, however, primarily concerned with getting their own job done. This was only natural, but the result was that the Marines were kept so busy on working parties that we could not carry out the training program we had planned.

We felt the training program was especially important because some of the Marines on Wake were recruits with only three or four months in the Corps, but we found ourselves unable to make more than a token gesture at training. I was ordered by Pearl Harbor to gather all gasoline drums on the island, clean them out and prepare to receive gasoline. A few days later, we found ourselves in the filling station business. Flights of B-17's were going through rather regularly en route to the Philippines, and since little provision had been made for servicing them at Wake, the Marines had to take on the job.

Tankers lying offshore were able to pump their

loads of gasoline to storage tanks on the island. Then Marine work parties, using small power pumps, emptied the big tanks into 50-gallon drums and carted the drums to fuel dumps which we scattered about in brush-hidden spots as a precaution in case of attack.

When the B-17's arrived, the Marines had to act as refueling crews. We had a gasoline truck we could use in servicing the planes, but in order to gas the planes quickly enough, the Marines also had to carry 50-gallon drums back to the airfield and pump their contents into the planes. There were times, such as when a tanker arrived to discharge its cargo, that the Marines worked in shifts right through a 24-hour period on this filling station duty.

Frankly, it did not make sense to me. None of my men was ground crew personnel. We were artillery-men—that was why we were on Wake Island—but the gasoline business did not leave us much time to work at our trade. For the most part, any training we were able to give on Wake was entirely incidental. For instance, if Marines working on a gun position saw a passing ship they might knock off work and track it for practice, but that method of training is not the most highly effective that might be devised. It was, however, about all we had time for. Of course, the fact that we were in the gas business did not affect the ultimate outcome of the battle for Wake Island, but it is equally true that we would have been better prepared for the fight if we could have used our time for the job we were sent to do.

As senior officer on Wake, one of my duties was to meet the clipper and welcome any dignitaries who might be passing through. Thus I met Saburo Kurusu on his way to Washington for those conferences the Japanese kept going as a smoke screen until the day they struck Pearl Harbor.

I had had a dispatch that Kurusu would be on the eastbound Clipper and that I should extend him all courtesy. The dispatch said he had no passport, but that this irregularity should be waived. So I was waiting as Mr. Kurusu, short and stockily plump, came up the ramp from the Clipper. Treading on his heels came his secretary, clutching a bulging briefcase as though afraid that somebody would snatch it from him.

I saluted and introduced myself. Mr. Kurusu was frigidly formal, "I suppose you have come to tell me that I can't leave the hotel?"

I replied, "No, sir, but you understand how these things are. None of the passengers may leave the vicinity of the hotel without special permission."

I escorted him to the hotel with the secretary tagging at our coattails. We sat in the lobby and ordered drinks. Mr. Kurusu began to thaw. He said he would stick to Scotch and soda—"I became accustomed to it in the Philippines many years ago."

He spoke such perfect English that if you had not been looking at him, you would not have known you were listening to a Japanese. I don't know whether his secretary spoke English or not. He didn't open his mouth. He just sat there—a cartoonist's idea of a Japanese schoolboy, blinking like an owl through his thick glasses and clutching that fantastic briefcase. I half expected it to pop open like an overstuffed sausage. The nearest he came to taking a part in our conversation was to shake his head when I asked if he would have a drink.

That made Mr. Kurusu laugh. He said, "He's just a young boy. He can't take it like older people."

As we sat there chatting over our drinks, I wondered what was going on behind his friendly eyes. I still do.

He said he had left on his mission at such short notice that he had had time to pack only one small bag, that he had practically no clothes except the pin-striped business suit he was wearing. And he did have a request to make:

"Please, I don't want to be bothered by the press."

I told him he was perfectly safe from reporters on Wake.

"In Manila," he said, "I was swamped by the press. And what could I tell them? I could talk only about the weather."

Mr. Kurusu insisted on paying for every round of drinks. Each time he said, "I have ample funds to take care of things like this."

All the time we sat there, perhaps an hour, we skirted around the one topic that must have been uppermost in both our minds. Only twice did he touch on it, and then each time he reminded me that he was married to an American of Japanese descent.

Once he agreed with me that if people could travel more and so come to know each other in their home countries, "perhaps these things would not come up."

And a little later, "I am just going to Washington to see what I can do. I hope I can straighten out affairs and avoid trouble."

After he got to San Francisco, we heard on the radio that Mr. Kurusu said, "I am here to try to prevent war."

He may have known even as he said it that Japan was determined on war. He may have known as we sat with our highballs on Wake Island that the conferences in Washington were only diplomatic double-talk to get us off our guard. I do not know, of course. But I felt in talking to him that he hoped sincerely to avoid trouble between the United States and Japan. It is still my feeling that Mr. Kurusu, personally, was not in favor of the war.

A lot of other passengers went through Wake in those last few weeks before the war—generals going to Iraq, Cairo or Washington; a family of Jews being evacuated from the Near East; an admiral going to the Philippines. Vincent Sheean went through, but I had to do the honors for some dignitary and so I did not meet him.

Then there was an important Englishman and his

wife. He was worried about where he would stay in Washington because he had heard of the shortage of hotel rooms. He finally decided, "I think Lord Halifax will put me up at the Embassy. After all, I put him up when he was through Burma."

As we drove around the island, I remarked, "We're trying to get ready as fast as we can."

The English dignitary's wife said, "Yes, it would be nice to have six months more, wouldn't it?"

I waited for him to make some comment, but he only nodded. I wondered what his wife might know; what he might have told her, but naturally I could not ask. News broadcasts from the States and occasional comments dropped by personages passing through on the Clipper were about the only information we had on which to estimate how tense the international crisis had become, and usually we were too busy to listen to the broadcasts. I did not worry about it, though. I felt that our government would be as well informed as any individual and that naturally we should be warned as soon as the international situation became acute enough to make danger to Wake imminent.

As far as I remember, however, I received only one official message on this subject while I was on Wake. The message came from Pearl Harbor in November. It said:

> International situation indicates you should
> be on the alert.

Ordinarily, on receiving such a message, I would have stopped routine construction and put all available men to work on defense installations. On, Wake, however, it was not for me to touch the contractor's men. So I sent back a priority query to Pearl Harbor. I asked:

> Does international situation indicate
> employment of contractor's men on de-

fense installations which are far from complete?

I felt certain I would get an immediate reply and I called a conference with Commander Greey and Mr. Teters. They were both wholly cooperative. We began figuring on work gangs and equipment which could be switched to such defense work as bomb shelters and revetments to protect the planes we assumed would be rushed to Wake if the situation were as acute as the message indicated. We delayed actually transferring any civilian crews to defense work pending the reply we expected hourly. The reply came two days later. It was negative. The tardiness of the reply made that negative even stronger in our minds, and we all felt a great deal easier about the outlook.

However, I was still apprehensive enough about the situation to increase the number of observation stations around the island. When I took command on Wake, I had moved ammunition to all gun positions and had placed rifle ammunition in each tent so that the men could fight their way to their positions if they were cut off by a sudden landing. Now I ordered more ammunition moved out to the gun positions.

In hindsight I believe that the decision made at the 14th Naval District Headquarters (Pearl Harbor) not to direct the contractor's men to work on defense installations was wrong. In the first place, it lulled us into a false sense of security. More important, the construction of such basic defense fixtures as revetments to protect the planes which we expected to arrive at any time would have contributed more to our defense of the island than did continuation of work on housing and so on. The decision reflects the influence at Pearl Harbor of the Civil Engineers of the Navy. In my opinion this influence was greater than the hard facts of the military situation warranted.

It was in November also that Commander Samuel P.

Ginder arrived in the seaplane tender *Curtiss* to bring us more gasoline and to look over the situation for Admiral Bellinger, who commanded the Patrol Wings operating from Pearl Harbor. Bad weather caught me aboard the *Curtiss* and I had to remain five days, but I kept in touch by radio with the officer I had left in charge ashore.

While I was aboard, the ship's radar picked up a flight of B-17's. We were supposed to have radar on Wake, but it had not arrived. So if the *Curtiss* had not been there with its radar, we would not have known that those B-17's had missed the island. We would not have known they were flying on, with little fuel left and Guam twelve hundred miles ahead.

I had to make a snap decision. On Wake, the radio homing signal was kept silent except to guide in the regular Clippers. The Japs knew the Clipper schedule, so the signal could tell them nothing new, but we did not want to take a chance of tipping them off that other planes were going through. Now I had to take the chance. I sent word to Pan-American Airways to open the homing signal, and so the lost B-17's were brought safely back to Wake for their vital refueling.

I was surprised to find that Commander Ginder had not been informed we were in the gasoline business nor even that the B-17's were passing through Wake on their way to the Philippines. He could not leave the ship, but when the weather abated he sent officers ashore with me to inspect the island, and I explained our whole situation to them. I pointed out, for instance, that plans called for construction of concrete emplacements for our guns, but that none had been built. The Marines had been forced to build their own makeshift artillery emplacements with twelve-by-twelve timbers, crossed and recrossed, and buried in the ground. Before Commander Ginder left, he knew how little we had and how seriously the gasoline business had interfered with our work on defense installations as well as our training program.

After Commander Ginder returned to Pearl Harbor and made his report, we finally began getting reinforcements of various kinds, about ten days before the war began.

At that time Commander Winfield Scott Cunningham arrived as Commanding Officer of the naval air station, which had been officially established though there were still no planes. As CO of the air station, Commander Cunningham took over as Island Commander while I remained in command of the Marine detachment. Commander Cunningham brought with him a supply officer and some clerical personnel and set up his headquarters in Camp Two, the civilian camp. (All ranks given are those held during the battle of Wake. Commander Cunningham has since been promoted to Captain and upon retirement to Rear Admiral. Most of the Wake Island Marines, officers and men, were also promoted.)

Commander Campbell Keene also arrived, bringing Navy ground personnel to establish the base for patrol planes and to command these Navy planes when they came to Wake.

We finally got planes four days before the war began, but they were only fighters—twelve F4F's of Marine Fighting Squadron 211. They were commanded by Major Paul A. Putnam, with whom I had served in Nicaragua when we were both second lieutenants in the same company. I was delighted to see him on Wake because I knew him well as an able, level-headed, cooperative officer. The decision to send the planes to Wake had been so secret that some of the pilots had boarded the aircraft carrier *Enterprise* with only extra skivvies and a toothbrush. On the second day at sea, they had learned they would not have a chance to go back for their luggage because they were bound for Wake as pilots of a dozen F4F's. The F4F was strange to the Marines, and for the next few days they had crammed under Navy instructors. When they were near enough to Wake, they took off and the *Enterprise* turned back toward Hawaii.

F4F's are Grumman Wildcats. They are fast, short-range fighters, of little value for scouting, but they were the only planes we had and so they had to serve as patrol planes, too. The morning after the squadron arrived, we began daily dawn and dusk patrols around the island. Commander Cunningham designated me to coordinate the activities of the defense battalion and our aircraft.

The various reinforcements we received during the last ten days of peace brought the total of military on Wake to 519. By far the largest group was my Marine detachment—15 officers and 364 men, including the Navy doctor and the hospital corpsmen attached to our unit.

Marine Fighting Squadron 211 had a dozen officers and 49 men, including Major Walter Bayler, who came to Wake on a special mission to set up a system of radio communication between the ground and planes in the air. The squadron's ground personnel reached the island a few days before the pilots brought in the planes.

The Navy had 11 officers and 64 men. These included the bluejackets of the small boat's crews, and hospital corpsmen and medical officer attached to my command.

The Army also had a detail on Wake—five enlisted men under Captain Henry S. Wilson. They had been sent to Wake with a radio truck to assist in communications for the Army planes passing through to the Philippines.

As welcome and badly needed as the reinforcements were, we were still hampered by lack of men and materiel. With the weapons and men and time at our disposal, however, we had set up the best defense we could devise, both against air attack or a landing.

We had planes at last, but we discovered that the only bombs we had on the island would not fit the bombracks of the only planes we had. The problem was solved by improvisation, which somebody defined as the basic industry of Wake Island. Marine mechanics stripped the supporting bands from water-filled practice bombs and put these bands on our only live bombs, the old style 100-pounders. Thus they were able to hook two live bombs onto each plane. Captain Herbert C. Freuler, the squadron's gunnery and ordnance officer, managed to have the makeshift bombholders in use a day or so before the war caught us.

That was typical of our situation on Wake, but some of our problems could not be solved by improvisation. They were simply facts about which we could do nothing.

For instance: None of Major Putnam's pilots had had more than thirty hours in Grumman Wildcats. None had ever dropped a bomb or fired a machine gun from that type of plane. The planes themselves had no armor, no leakproof gasoline tanks, no radio homing equipment.

We had the artillery of a full defense battalion—three 5-inch batteries (two guns each) and three 3-inch antiaircraft batteries (four guns each)—a total of eighteen guns. But we literally did not have half enough Marines to man those six batteries, as well as our machine guns, in combat. The bare training allowance of a defense battalion at that time was about 850 men. We had 378 to do a battalion's job.

In two of the 3-inch batteries, we were able to man only three of each battery's four guns. We had nobody who could be spared from other duties to serve a single gun in the third 3-inch battery. In terms of lost fire power, our shortage of personnel added up to this: we had a total of twelve 3-inch AA guns and we could man only six of them. We were never able to bring into effective action more than a part of the machine guns we had, twenty-four .50 caliber for AA fire and thirty .30 caliber for ground defense.

We were able to man all our 5-inch guns, but only one battery of any kind on Wake had its full training allowance. Godbold's 3-inch battery had its full training complement of sixty-two men and two officers. At that time, incidentally, the Army allowed 140 men and four officers for a battery with virtually the same weapons.

We were shorthanded not only in the gun crews but in the communications section and every other group in the battalion. My staff was typical. Major George H. Potter, Jr. was my executive officer. He was also my adjutant, my operations officer, my intelligence officer and my supply officer. He was my whole staff—and group commander of the 5-inch batteries.

Lack of personnel was only part of the picture. We were desperately short of equipment, too. Even with full gun crews, one entire 3-inch battery would still have been useless because we had no fire control equipment for it. Only one of the 3-inch batteries had complete fire control equipment. The other partly manned battery did not have a height-finder, which put it pretty much in the position of a boxer trying to fight blindfolded. We kept this battery in action, however, by having the essential data telephoned from the battery that had our only height-finder. Fortunately, our 5-inch batteries did have sufficient fire control equipment at the start, but there was little or no equipment for replacement of damaged parts.

We were even short of oil releases, a gadget by which the crew of a 3-inch AA gun can release the pressure so that they can change the recoil oil, which is necessary if the gun is to be kept functioning properly. Each gun crew was supposed to have an oil release and each battery was supposed to have a spare. For our three AA batteries, we should have had fifteen of these important gadgets. We had two.

Each Marine had his rifle and bayonet, of course, but the Navy and Army personnel had been sent to Wake without rifles, gas masks or helmets. Even the officers lacked sidearms. I suppose that when they were sent to Wake, somebody took it for granted they would draw weapons and gear at their new station, but neither the

Navy nor Army had any such equipment on Wake for them to draw.

Then there was our radar. We were expecting it on every ship, but it had not arrived. We had to depend on the men at our observation stations and lookouts on the two 50-foot steel water towers, the highest structures on the island. Our own eyes and ears were the only detection devices we had.

It seems that our radar equipment was crated and sitting for some time on the dock in Hawaii for shipment. Shipment was delayed, apparently because cargo related to the construction of the Wake Island air installation had a higher priority. As the situation developed, it must be apparent to everyone that the radar equipment would have been far more important in the defense of the island than any construction materials could have possibly been.

This lack of men and equipment made the problem of Wake Island rather more difficult than it might have been. The small area of the atoll is apt to be misleading unless one realizes that it has a coastline, including the lagoon, almost twenty miles long. Our problem becomes clearer if one considers that this coastline we had to defend was about equal to a line running from Washington halfway to Baltimore. Even if we could have manned all the machine guns we had on the island, we would have had less than one machine gun for each quarter-mile of beach we had to defend.

Under such circumstances, it would have been ridiculous to think we might hold the island against an all-out attack. Nor were we expected to. Before I left Pearl Harbor, the question had been discussed at length with Colonel Harry Pickett and Lieutenant Colonel Omar T. Pfeiffer. Colonel Pfeiffer was an Assistant Operations Officer on the staff of Rear Admiral Husband E. Kimmel, commanding the Pacific Fleet. Colonel Pickett, commanding Marine Barracks, Navy Yard, had additional duties on the staff of Admiral C.C. Bloch as coordinator of the defense battalions sent out from Pearl Harbor. Admiral Bloch commanded the Sea Frontier as well as the Hawaii naval district.

Colonel Pickett and Lieutenant Colonel Pfeiffer agreed that the mission of the Marines on Wake was only to withstand a "minor raid," a hit-and-run attack such as German raiders made against some of the British islands in the Pacific during World War I. A raider would show up, shell the island and put ashore a landing party to obtain supplies, destroy installations, or both. It was felt we were strong enough to repulse such a raid, or even a considerably stronger raid after we had been reinforced, but it was not contemplated that we would be able to withstand a full-scale attack. If such an attack were thrown at us, however, we were expected to do the best we could.

I don't think any of us worried about it. Morale was high on Wake that last weekend before the war. I remember that it was the only good weekend since I had landed on the island. That Saturday I had been able for the first time to give the whole detachment a dummy run on general quarters, sending all units to their positions as though we were being attacked. I was pleased with the snap and speed of the drill, especially since we had been able to make only a gesture at a training program. After the drill, being caught up for the moment with our extra-Marine duties, I was able to give the men Saturday afternoon off, the first they'd had since I took command.

The next day was the second Sunday they'd had off in more than two months. As Wake lies west of the International Date Line, it is a day later there than in Hawaii and the States. So Sunday, December 7, on Wake Island was only Saturday, December 6, in Pearl Harbor.

The men fished, swam, loafed or possibly engaged in certain games of chance. I do not know what they did with their spare time because I feel an officer has no right to ride herd on his men when they are off duty. I still follow the only advice my father, an Army officer, gave me when I became a second lieutenant, "When your men are off duty—for God's sake leave 'em alone!" I do remember that a couple of lieutenants, Wally Lewis and Barney Barninger, celebrated the holiday by capsizing their little sailboat.

The Clipper arrived that day with mail from the States and moored for an overnight stop before continuing the flight to Guam. The gossip the passengers brought and the news we heard on the radio were neither better nor worse than they had been. Most of us expected war sooner or later, but we had heard "Wolf! Wolf!" cried for so many years that we didn't bother much about it. If we had time to get ready, well and good. If we didn't, we'd have to make-do with what we had. Meanwhile, there was no use fretting, because if you weren't stationed on this island, you'd be stationed on some other one. I think that was the way most of us felt on Wake the last night of peace.

As I walked back to my tent that night, it occurred to me that I had been quite a prophet the last time I had seen my brother Ashton. I had gone on leave from San Diego in January, 1941, to see my people in Washington. The day I arrived, I was ordered to return at once to my post. My brother, driving me to the station, wondered what the sudden orders meant.

I said, "Oh, I'll probably wind up on some little spit-kit of an island."

It was amusing to remember this later, on Wake Island. But I did not know then, that last night before the war, just how good a prophet I had really been. For when Ashton asked me what I thought would happen, I had replied:

"Your guess is as good as mine—but I'll probably wind up eating fish and rice."

Just before we were attacked it was my good fortune as a commanding officer to execute papers which tùrned out to be of great benefit to two of my personnel. First, I executed orders promoting Harold C. Borth from NCO to the rank of Marine Gunner. This gave Borth officer status through the long four years in prison camp. Second, I executed adoption papers for my executive officer, Major Potter. His wife was then able to adopt an infant son to keep her company for the years that her husband was away. Had these two actions been delayed the papers could not have been executed until our release from prison camp at the end of the war.

Chapter Two

The Attack

IT BEGAN LIKE ANY OTHER Monday morning on Wake Island. As I shaved, I could see men ambling to breakfast or puttering around their tents. It was not quite seven, and the men were taking it easy, getting squared away for the day. Then Captain Wilson burst into my tent with the news that Pearl Harbor had been attacked. His Army radio truck had intercepted an uncoded message from Hawaii. He thrust it at me:

> Hickham Field has been attacked by Jap
> dive bombers! This is the real thing.

I remember I rinsed my face and reached for a towel. Then I telephoned Commander Cunningham's quarters, but I couldn't reach him. I called the Navy radio shack and asked if they had received a priority message from Pearl Harbor.

"Yes, sir. It's being decoded now."

That was verification enough for me. I started for my office about fifty yards away. As I passed the guard tent, I told them to send me the Music on the double. First Sergeant Paul Agar was already at his desk when I walked into the temporary building that served as my office.

"It's started," I said. "The Japs have attacked

Pearl Harbor."

He gaped at me. Then:

"Well, I'll be god-damned."

The bugler ran in. I ordered, "Sound call to arms." Some of the men were eating, some were policing around the tents, and two or three officers were strolling over for a tardy breakfast when the bugle sounded. Nobody believed it. They took it for just another dummy run. They were laughing, joking, skylarking as they went for their rifles and gear. Some of them tried to gobble the last of their breakfast as the trucks rolled up to take them to the guns.

I stood outside my office, watching. Some of the men were not bothering to lug along the emergency rifle ammunition I had ordered to each tent. I shouted to them:

"This is no drill! Pass the word!"

Some bolted for the ammunition and then scrambled for the trucks. Some stood gawking a moment before it sank in. They were moving now. On the double. The word was passing. *"This is no drill!"* Some were half-dressed, but they didn't wait to finish. They were piling in the trucks, and the trucks were rolling now. This was what we'd been waiting for. We'd been talking about it for years. Now here it was. The chips were down. It seemed to me, watching, as though an electric current passed through the island.

Commander Cunningham stopped at my office. He had passed the trucks going to the gun positions. He said, "I see you already know . . . . Anything I can do?"

"I don't know of anything right now."

His Command Post would be at Camp Two, he said. I told him I would move my CP into the brush as soon as we could set up a switchboard.

The batteries were reporting now. In less than forty-five minutes after Captain Wilson had burst into my tent, I received the report "manned and ready" from my last position.

We were almost swamped at the office. People kept crowding in with questions that had to be answered right away, with problems that had to be solved at once. What about bomb shelters and caches for supplies? How would we keep the positions scattered all over the island supplied with food and water? And we had to get extra ammunition to all positions. Some of the batteries were not fully sandbagged. We'd need more sandbags and we'd need work crews to repair the damage when the enemy struck. Communications had to be checked. Alternate lines had to be laid. When the Japs came, we couldn't expect our phone lines to be bombproof.

What about the sailors and the five soldiers? They had no weapons of any kind, no gas masks, not even helmets. We had a small store of rifles which we used for spare parts. I ordered these arms issued to as many as we could supply. Sidearms were issued to some of the naval officers. We had no helmets or gas masks to give them. If the Japs used gas, it would be just too bad.

Another question: We had a sickbay at Camp One, and the civilians had a larger hospital with a civilian doctor at Camp Two; Lieutenant (jg) Gustav M. Kahn, our Navy doctor, wanted to know if he should take over the civilian hospital which was under a civilian physician, Dr. Lawton Ely Shark. I said he should.

"I just wanted to have it straight," he said.

A moment later, I looked up and saw a civilian at my CP. He was standing rigidly at attention.

"Sir," he said, "Adams, former seaman United States Navy, reporting for duty. Sir, can you use me?"

We could. We needed everybody we could get for non-combat labor, for the work parties Dan Teters began rounding up for us as soon as he heard that war had started. Marines were in work parties, too, but I ordered all battery commanders to keep at least one gun fully manned at all times. Marines of the other gun crews might be used to strengthen positions, build shelters and cache ammunition and chow, but they should be used only for tasks in the battery area.

My batteries were paired off, a 3-inch with a 5-inch, and emplaced near the island's three extremities—Peacock, Kuku and Toki points. The guns of the crewless 3-inch battery were near Toki Point. On each of the islands of the atoll and around the airfield, .50 caliber machine guns were emplaced as additional anti-aircraft armament. Beach defense was provided by .30 caliber machine guns set up at strategic points all around the island.

One thing happened that morning that is hard to put in words. Field Music Alvin Waronker had never wanted to be a bugler. He had volunteered for Music School in the States because that seemed the only way he could avoid being shipped to Alaska and he didn't like cold weather. He tried hard, but it was rather plain from the first that he was never intended to be a bugler. This seemed especially obvious when he tried to sound Colors. No matter how hard he tried, it always came out sour. His vain struggles with that call were something of a battalion joke.

Morning Colors is at 8:00 a.m. on a Marine post, and this morning we heard something none of us will ever be able to explain. I doubt even Waronker could. He just stood there and sounded off as the flag went up, and every note was proud and clear. It made a man's throat tighten to hear it. This time there were no wisecracks when the last note ended. It was the only time it ever happened, but that once Field Music Waronker was top of the heap.

Meanwhile, in the Army radio trailer, Sergeant James Rex was trying desperately to persuade the Australian operators in Darwin and in Port Moresby, New Guinea, that the Japs really had attacked Pearl Harbor. He kept telling them to notify their officers, and they kept telling him to quit his kidding. He finally had to give up. He reported that the Philippines said they could not get in communication with the States and so the trailer on Wake had become a relay point.

At the airfield, Major Putnam's squadron was as busy as everybody else, with their own particular headaches. In his four days on the island, he had put as many men as he could spare to building revetments and wooden platforms out from the strip onto the soft coral so the planes could warm up without being bunched on the strip. Another group was improvising tie-down stakes so the planes could be dispersed more widely than if they used the tie-down mat already constructed. But these tasks were only getting started. There had been too little time. A bulldozer had been made available to work on the revetments and it was thought that these could be ready by midafternoon.

The news of Pearl Harbor reached the airfield as the two-plane morning patrol was about to take off. Putnam's first order was to increase the patrol to four planes. He ordered that four planes should be kept in the air at all times, by operating in relays, with four standing by as relief and the remaining four planes out for maintenance. Then he led off our first patrol of the war while his men at the airfield dug foxholes and redoubled their efforts to finish run-offs and revetments before the enemy could attack. Major Putnam was confronted with a dilemma which he later described:

"The Squadron Commander was faced with a choice between two major decisions, and inevitably he chose the wrong one. Work was progressing simultaneously on six of the protective bunkers for the airplanes, and while none was available for immediate occupancy, all would be ready not later than by 1400. Protection and camouflage for facilities were not available but could be made ready within 24 hours. Foxholes or other prepared positions for personnel did not exist but would be completed not later than 1400. To move the airplanes out of the regular parking area entailed grave risk of

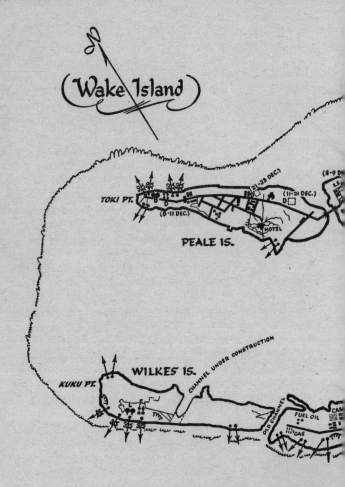

Wake Island

TOKI PT.

(8-11 DEC.)

21-23 DEC.

(11-21 DEC.)

(8-9 De...)

HOTEL

PEALE IS.

WILKES IS.

CHANNEL UNDER CONSTRUCTION

KUKU PT.

OLD CHANNEL

FUEL OIL

CAM...

GAS

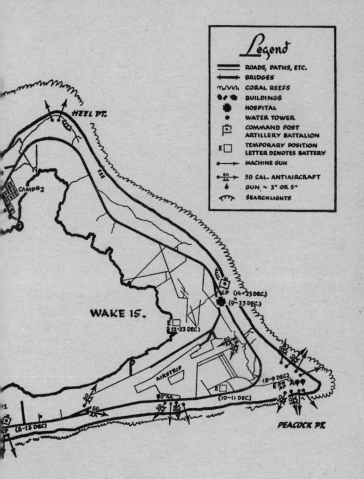

Legend

═══	ROADS, PATHS, ETC.
	BRIDGES
∿∿∿	CORAL REEFS
	BUILDINGS
	HOSPITAL
●	WATER TOWER
	COMMAND POST ARTILLERY BATTALION
E ▢	TEMPORARY POSITION LETTER DENOTES BATTERY
→	MACHINE GUN
50 AA	50 CAL. ANTIAIRCRAFT GUN ~ 3" OR 5"
	SEARCHLIGHTS

HEEL PT.

CAMP #2

WAKE IS.

CP (14-23 DEC.)
(9"-23 DEC.)

E ▢
(12-23 DEC.)

AIRSTRIP

E ▢
(10-11 DEC.)

(8-9 DEC.)
E 5"

3"AA

(8-13 DEC.)

PEACOCK PT.

damage, and damage meant complete loss of an airplane because of the complete absence of spare parts . . . . The Squadron Commander decided to avoid certain damage to his airplanes by moving them across the rough ground, to delay movements of material until someplace could be prepared to receive it, and to trust his personnel to take natural cover if attacked.''

Putnam's patrol saw no sign of enemy aircraft or surface vessels. He returned to the field about 9:30 a.m. Captain Henry Elrod led off the four-plane relief as patrol commander.

The Pan-American Clipper had departed for Guam at daylight, but a flash from Pearl Harbor brought it back to Wake. Now the skipper, Captain John H. Hamilton, of Texarkana, Arkansas, volunteered to take his big ship on a wide patrol if we would give him a fighter escort.

I went to the airfield to discuss the Clipper patrol with commander Cunningham, Major Putnam and Captain Hamilton. We gave Captain Hamilton the approach he should make returning to the island and decided the approximate time he should return so that my gunners would be expecting him. I didn't want to take any chances that some gun crew might mistake the Clipper for a Jap and shoot it down. Commander Cunningham decided that the Clipper, escorted by two fighters, would take off after lunch and make a search for a hundred miles around the island.

As the situation developed, the search directed by Commander Cunningham was never conducted, and the Clipper took off for Midway at 12:50, evacuating certain Pan-American personnel plus all passengers— except Mr. H.P. Hevenor, a government official who missed the plane, was marooned on Wake, and eventually ended up in Japanese hands.

I went back to my office. I made a phone check of all positions. Everything was in hand. The lookouts on the water towers reported all clear. Lacking radar, we had no way of knowing that twenty-seven Japanese bombers were bearing down on us.

Even the weather was with them.

Our four-plane patrol was above the cloud ceiling and so could not spot the Jap bombers coming in below it.

A rain squall was sweeping in on the island, and the Japs came in behind it, hidden from view until they were on top of us.

Nobody heard them. The surf on the reefs around the island made it hard to hear motors, but even so the Japs took no chances. They cut off their motors and came down on us in a silent glide behind the mask of the squall.

It was 11:50 a.m.

At the Pan-American Hotel, the Clipper passengers were lunching and wondering how badly Pearl Harbor had been hit.

At the airfield, eight planes were on the strip. Until the run-offs were finished, planes could not be dispersed out of the parking area without blocking the runway or being moved over rough ground at a risk of almost certain damage. Mechanics were making four planes ready to relieve the patrol in the air. Two more were being warmed up to escort the Clipper.

First Lieutenant George A. Graves and Second Lieutenant Robert Conderman were assigned to escort the Clipper. They were being briefed in the ready tent. Most of the other pilots were there, too.

I was on the telephone in my office. I was giving some routine instructions to Lieutenant Wally Lewis at Peacock Point when he suddenly broke in:

"Major, there's a squadron of planes coming in from the south. Are they friendly?"

It was 11:58.

The gliding bombers were almost on top of us when they broke out of the rain squall at barely two thousand feet. A civilian yelled, "Look! Their wheels are falling off!" Only it wasn't wheels. Over the phone, Lewis was yelling, "They're dropping bombs!"

The next instant, I heard the first bombs exploding.

Lewis' battery opened up, but the Japs were too close aboard and coming in too low for effective 3-inch fire.

The .50's were blasting as the bombers crossed the beachline in waves between Camp One and Peacock Point, but nothing was stopping the Japs today. They headed straight for the airfield, passing hardly fifteen hundred feet above our heads, spraying their path with machine gun fire. They turned that strip into a slab of hell.

Technically, the enemy covered the entire working area of the airfield with a closely spaced pattern of fragmentation bombs and intense machine gun fire. That means the Japs caught the planes on the ground like sitting ducks. It means the men on the ground didn't have a chance.

The big tank—twenty-five thousand gallons of gasoline—went up in flaming waste. Several hundred drums of gasoline were burning, too, in the shattered wake of the bombers. In that wake were only the dead and wounded and wreckage. Some of the wounded were moaning. Some were trying to crawl away. Some were sitting up, dazed, trying to stop the blood that wouldn't stop. And the second wave of bombers was coming in.

Some of the pilots tried to reach their planes, gambling for a chance to get into the air to give battle. They were running through strafing fire, and one fell—Second Lieutenant Frank Holden, cut to pieces by bullets. Second Lieutenant Harry G. Webb was shot in the stomach and both feet crippled. The bombs were dropping again.

Graves and Conderman kept running. Graves made it. He climbed in his plane, but it never had a chance to move. A bomb got it. A direct hit.

Conderman, son of a Marine Officer, was almost close enough to his plane to touch it when a Jap machine-gunned him. He fell. He couldn't crawl away. Men ran to help him.

"Let me go," he said.

He was dying. He tried to point to wounded men scattered beyond him.

"Take care of them," he said.

As the bombers finished their pass across the atoll, droning off out to sea, nine or ten of them swung back for a run at Peale Island.

They plastered the Pan-American station with bombs, slashed across the island with strafing fire, and left a flame-dotted shambles in their path. The company's radio station, the machine shop and other buildings were destroyed. Fuel tanks were set afire. A direct hit killed ten of the company's employees, all Chamorros from Guam, and others were wounded. The hotel was badly battered, and the Japs strafed the Clipper at its dock, puncturing it with scores of bullets.

The Toki Point guns threw up ack-ack, but again the enemy came in too low for effective 3-inch fire. They were barely fifteen hundred feet up as they made their run. Maybe our .50's got some hits, but we saw no sign of any. The Japs had it all their own way.

While VMF-211's combat air patrol had been making a swing north of Wake at 12,000 feet, half a mile below them the 36 twin-tailed Japanese bombers had approached the atoll and made their gliding letdown into the squall at 2,000 feet.

Then they were gone. The entire attack on both islands had lasted only ten minutes.

At the airfield, thirty-four men were dead or wounded. Seven of the planes caught on the ground had been destroyed. The auxiliary gas tank of the eighth plane was damaged beyond repair. When our four-plane patrol came down after the Japs were gone, the strip was so torn up by the bombing that one of the Wildcats broke its propeller in landing. Thus three quarters of our air power was knocked out by the enemy's first punch without getting a chance to strike a single blow in return.

While the attack was still going on, Major Putnam and his men tried desperately to rescue wounded and save equipment. Putnam was hit, then he was dazed by bomb concussion, but he wouldn't let them treat him. He was too busy leading the last forlorn hope of saving something from the ruin. Others, too, kept on, though wounded. Captain Frank C. Tharin was one. Staff Sergeant R. O. Arthur another. And the durable Sergeant Paszkiewicz, Master Technical Sergeant Andrew J. Paszkiewicz, a Marine for twenty years.

Sergeant Paszkiewicz was caught in the first blast at the airfield. Bomb fragments shattered his right leg. He caught a burst of bullets, too. He started crawling off, dragging his smashed leg limply behind him.

The second wave of bombers was coming in. Sergeant Paszkiewicz reached a pile of wreckage and began fumbling in it. He found what he wanted, a piece of wood. With a little fixing it could serve as a crutch. It didn't take him long.

The bombs were dropping again. Machine guns were chopping across the strip. Sergeant Paszkiewicz pulled himself upright and tried his crutch. He started hobbling off. He seemed to be going the wrong way. Instead of going to safety, he stumped stolidly back the way he had come. Somebody tried to help him, but Sergeant Paszkiewicz wasn't having any. Second Lieutenant David D. Kliewer saw him stumbling about on his makeshift crutch, giving first aid to the wounded or trying to make a dying man lie a little easier. For some of the Marines caught at the airfield, that was the most anybody could do.

Chapter Three

Afternoon, December 8

WE HAD TAKEN A BEATING and we knew that first raid was only a curtain raiser. We knew the Japs would come again and again until they bombed us into helplessness, or thought they had. Then they would come in for the kill. They would try to land troops from the sea or from the air or both. Perhaps we would be reinforced before then, as most of us expected, but we could not depend on it. We could depend only on ourselves, on our ability to make up by improvisation for our lack of men and equipment.

It was rather cold comfort that first afternoon of the war to realize that we had been all set for the Japs, manned and ready, and that they had caught us only because we did not have our radar. If we'd had our radar, even though the enemy did get all the breaks on the weather that day, all of Putnam's planes would have been in the air intercepting the Japs instead of some of them sitting on the ground like so many clay pipes in a shooting gallery.

Our radar equipment had been issued while I was still in Pearl Harbor. When I left for Wake, I was informed that it would be sent on to us. The plan called for a Navy radar station to be set up on Wake like that one that had been established on Midway, in addition to the detachments, but for some reason our equipment never arrived.

Commander Keene, who came to Wake to command the Navy patrol planes that never arrived, told me that he had seen our radar equipment on the dock in Hawaii, but neither he nor anyone else had ever informed me why it was not sent to us in the weeks that elapsed between the time I left Pearl Harbor and the day the Japs attacked. We received other equipment during that period. We got a garbage truck for instance. It was a useful vehicle, but it could not detect Jap bombers coming down on us out of a rain squall.

I have heard since that Admiral Kimmel wanted us to have the radar as planned, but that objections were raised against sending radar to a vulnerable spot for fear the Japanese might capture it and so learn one of our most important war secrets. Such an objection may have been well taken, but I believe we could have been depended upon to destroy the equipment before the enemy could capture it. That is, of course, merely my personal opinion.

In any case, we had neither radar nor our pre-radar listening horns on Wake. We never did have any kind of plane detection device.

Whatever might have happened if we'd had our radar, the simple fact remained that we had lost the first round of the battle for Wake Island. The enemy had hit us a staggering blow and escaped almost scot-free. The airfield area and the Pan-American station looked like burning junk yards. Except for one damaged plane and the radio shack, all of the squadron's equipment on the ground had been destroyed. Almost the only encouraging aspects of the squadron's situation were these: we still had three planes in flying condition and two merely damaged. The bombs in the sunken magazines had escaped destruction. We were not out of gas. Despite the loss of both storage tanks and one fuel dump in the airfield area, we still had plenty of gasoline in six widely scattered dumps in the brush.

Major Putnam's first task was to reorganize his riddled squadron. He had lost about half his personnel. Captain Tharin and some of the others still on duty were, like Putnam, carrying on despite wounds. We were too shorthanded on Wake for the slightly wounded to lay off.

The squadron did not have a single qualified mechanic left. The task of keeping the Wildcats flying was given to Second Lieutenant John F. Kinney and Technical Sergeant William J. Hamilton, an enlisted pilot. Every bit of the squadron's maintenance equipment had been destroyed, but Lieutenant Kinney and Sergeant Hamilton scouted the civilian camp and elsewhere for what they could find and set up shop. They performed miracles in improvisation, salvaging parts from wreckage to send crippled planes back into the air, switching parts back and forth from plane to plane as though making moves in some fantastic game of mechanical checkers. Often they worked all night to nurse into flight a plane that was no more than a scrap heap on wheels. In one of his last reports before the end, Major Putnam said of these two Marines:

"Ever since the first raid, they traded parts and assemblies back and forth until not one plane could be identified. They swapped engines, junked, stripped and rebuilt them, and all but created them. It is solely due to their efforts that the squadron is still operating."

Major Putnam's losses of men and planes forced him to abandon his plan for constant daylight patrols after the first attack. Instead, he ordered patrols flown at dawn, midday and dusk. That was the best he could do with what he had left.

Though the Pan-American Hotel was badly damaged, all the passengers had escaped injury when the Jap bombers interrupted their lunch. Examination revealed that the Clipper had escaped without any structural damage despite the scores of bullets that had struck it.

The captain dumped the mail to make room for as many of the personnel as possible and took off at 1:00 p.m.

The defense battalion came through the first raid without a single casualty, largely because the Japs were after different game that day.

But we had no time to celebrate this one piece of good luck. We were too busy. Communications lines bombed out in the first attack had to be replaced. Sandbag emplacements which had caved in under firing had to be repaired. Air raid shelters had to be constructed. Fresh supplies of water and ammunition had to be trucked out to the positions and distributed in caches in each battery area. As a precaution against losing our stock of food in a bombing attack, the civilians under Dan Teters, began that afternoon moving food stores to dumps scattered over the three islands. Some of the caches were hidden in the scrub, but others had to be camouflaged with brush or by covering them with sand and coral, depending on the nature of the surrounding terrain. If fresh vegetation is used for camouflage, it must be changed daily or the dying leaves will serve not as camouflage but as a giveaway, an invitation to the enemy to drop his bombs on that spot. All that meant hours of aching labor, day and night; weary, dirty grubbing that seemed to have no end.

The Marines and the handful of Navy personnel could not do all that had to be done. It could not have been done without Dan Teters' civilian workmen. With their heavy equipment, for instance, they could build a bomb shelter in a fraction of the time it would have taken Marines with pick and shovel. The saving in time meant lives saved because it meant that we had to take our chances in fewer raids without bomb shelters.

I stress this point because I feel that the movie *Wake Island* gave rise to a misconception about our fight that does Mr. Teters a grave injustice. You may remember that the contractor in the movie would not cooperate with the Marines. That is not at all the way it was. Big Dan Teters, ex-football star at the University of Washington, an Army sergeant in World War I, was one of the first on the island to volunteer help after the news of Pearl Harbor. Commander Greey was ill in the hospital, so we had to turn to Mr. Teters when we needed civilian work parties. From that first day, I would tell him what had to be done or how many men we needed for a job, and ex-Sergeant Teters never failed to come through, though frequently it took some tall doing.

Not all of the civilians helped us. Some of them took off into the brush when the first bomb fell and did not show themselves again until after the surrender. They took quantities of supplies, dug themselves shelters and sat out the battle. There were times when we needed them badly, and I was urged to send Marines into the brush to round them up, but I could not do it. I did not have the men to spare.

I record these facts simply because it is part of what happened and not because I believe the civilians who hid out should be judged harshly. One must take into consideration the fact that the civilians were not mentally prepared for the shock of war as were the Marines. One or two of my detachment had fought in the First World War and a larger group of us had seen service in Nicaragua, but even the greenest recruit had been conditioned from the day he went to boot camp to regard war as his trade. The attitude was: if you have to fight, that's just part of your job. The civilians had not been conditioned in this way, so it seems entirely understandable that many of them tried to hide from danger. In my view that only makes more admirable the action of those among them who turned to and stuck to the finish.

John Burroughs was typical. He was from Colorado, a cost accountant who had once worked for the FHA. He went to Peacock Point the first afternoon of the action at Wake as one of a work crew. Before the job was done, he was a leader in the crew. He led them in volunteering to stay at Peacock Point as a permanent detail instead of returning to their camp. Burroughs' volunteers stayed there through the rest of the battle, repairing bomb damage or doing anything else that came up, and they provided the entire ammunition-handling detail for the 5-inch battery at Peacock Point.

There were others, too. Jimmy Jamieson, a tireless genius with a bulldozer. Peter Russell and Rex Jones. Forsythe, a seaman in the old Navy. Harry Yeager, Doc Stevenson, Pete Sorenson. And a stammering little man called Fritz who was worried that the Marines might think he stammered because he was afraid. He kept explaining that he had always stammered.

Some of the civilians volunteered that first afternoon to relieve Marines on watches, but I ordered that no watch should be entrusted to civilians alone. The invariable rule was that on such watches as a civilian might stand, he must be paired with a Marine who would be responsible for the watch.

Quite a number of civilians had hung around with Marines, learning what they could about the various weapons. Now they wanted to fight. Ex-seaman Adams was only one of a number who came to my office the first day and wanted to join the Marines. Of sixteen civilians dispatched to Peale Island that afternoon, two were assigned to the director crew as lookouts and the rest were formed into a gun crew with a veteran Marine, Sergeant W.A. Bowsher, as gun captain. Otherwise, the crewless gun in the 3-inch battery on Peale could not have been brought into action.

It is a widespread misconception that it is always contrary to international law for civilians to serve as combatants. That is not the case. Under international law, civilians are justified in taking up arms in defense of their homes against an invasion. However, on Wake, civilians were generally restricted to activities which would not jeopardize their status as noncombatants.

One of our biggest problems was feeding the units dispersed over the three islands, especially since I needed Marines at combat posts too badly to spare them for mess duty. So Dan Teters took over the job of feeding us. My mess sergeants helped, but generally the preparation and distribution of food was handled by civilians. We had a considerable store of food on the island, but we did not know how long it might be before we would get more, so we began strict conservation of rations. We decided to feed only two meals a day.

By the end of the first day, as beach patrols began their night watch all along the shore, as work on installations continued in the darkness, a check of our positions made me feel we had done fairly well, with the time we had, in getting ready for the next attack.

The runway was mined with dynamite and connections for exploding it were made to three generators placed near machine gun positions around the airfield. The level ground around the strip had been turned into ridges by a bulldozer to prevent enemy planes from landing in case the Japs tried that method of getting troops on the island.

Second Lieutenant A. A. Poindexter was entrusted with the defense of Camp One, the small boat channel and the beach in that area. His small detachment was increased to seventy-three men by scraping together the bluejackets of the small boat's crews, and cooks, clerks and almost every other Marine who did not have an essential combat duty. We created a "mobile reserve" by putting four machine guns on a truck and assigning a dozen of Poindexter's qualified Marines to man it. These men were spread thinly among his motley force, standing their watches at night, acting as the core of his defense, until the mobile reserve should be needed. Then these designated men would be pulled out to man the truck and rush the four machine guns to whatever point might be threatened.

We strengthened all positions as much as possible, but did not change the location of the heavy batteries. In addition to Lieutenant Poindexter's detachment, my force was dispersed as follows. This dispersal should be kept in mind in order to follow the subsequent action:

PEACOCK POINT: 5-inch battery (two guns) commanded by First Lieutenant Clarence A. Barninger and 3-inch battery (three guns effective) commanded by First Lieutenant W. W. Lewis; with Lieutenant Barninger as strongpoint commander.

TOKI POINT: 5-inch battery (two guns) commanded by First Lieutenant Woodrow M. Kessler and 3-inch battery (four guns) commanded by Captain Bryghte D. Godbold; with Captain Godbold as Peale Island strongpoint commander. The fourth gun in Godbold's battery was manned by Sergeant Bowsher and his civilian volunteers.

KUKU POINT: 5-inch battery (two guns) commanded by Second Lieutenant J.A. McAlister; with Captain W.M. Platt as Wilkes Island strongpoint commander. My third 3-inch battery (four guns) was emplaced on Wilkes, but this battery had no personnel and no fire control equipment.

AIRFIELD: Machine guns, .50's and .30's, spotted around the strip and manned by nineteen Marines under Second Lieutenant R.M. Hanna.

In addition, four .50's were emplaced for A.A. fire on Wilkes Island, four at Peacock Point and four on Peale. Each strongpoint commander also had .30's for ground defense.

Heel Point was defended by nine Marines commanded by a corporal. They had their rifles and two .30 caliber machine guns.

I put two .30's on Kuku Point and two on Toki Point, covering the entrance to the lagoon in case the enemy tried to slip in that way in rubber boats. The lagoon entrance is about a mile and a quarter wide, which I realized was too wide to be covered adequately by observation, but there was nothing more I could do about it.

I mentioned that only one of our 3-inch batteries had a height-finder. That was Godbold's battery on Peale, and the data had to be telephoned to Lewis at Peacock Point. I had nobody to man the 3-inch battery on Wilkes.

Major Potter was still my entire staff, but two warrant officers were now working out of my CP. Marine Gunner John Hamas served as munitions officer, the man who had to keep the guns supplied with ammunition. Marine Gunner H.C. Borth was my trouble shooter on the guns.

During the night, after the overworked communications men got a switchboard hooked up, I moved my CP out into the brush. It was dank and unpleasant, but we were concealed there. Nobody got any sleep. Marines and civilian volunteers worked on the defenses all night.

Over on Peale Island, as night fell, Pfc Verne L. Wallace got a letter he had been worrying about all day. It was from his girl back in Haverford, Pennsylvania.

The letter had arrived on the Clipper, but Pfc Wallace had been on guard duty when the mail was passed out. He was told a friend had picked up the letter for him. Pfc Wallace was walking to his friend's tent to get the letter when call to arms sounded. After that, he was too busy. He had a gun to man against the Jap attack. Then there was work to be done getting ready for the next attack. It was night before he happened to bump into his friend on a work party, and then it was too dark to read it. But in the first dim light of morning, dog-weary from a night of labor, at long last he opened his letter. Just as the order passed to man the guns for the dawn alert, Pfc Wallace read:

"As long as you have to be away, darling, I'm so very, very happy you are in the Pacific where you won't be in danger if war comes."

Brigadier General James P.S. Devereux, USMC (Ret.)

BEFORE THE WAR: The Pan-American Airways station was on Peale Island, with a small modern hotel *(top)*, its own radio station, shop buildings, and landing dock *(bottom)* where the Clipper moored in the lagoon. Established in 1935, the station was a refueling stop for two Clippers weekly, one eastbound, the other westbound.

DEFENDERS: *(Top)* Lt. Arthur Poindexter of Huntington Beach, Calif.; Pfc Eugene Lutz *(bottom)*, now a Catholic priest in McHenry, Ill.; and Pfc James King of Foster City, Calif.

UPI Photos

A reenactment of Japanese troops storming ashore, as portrayed in Paramount Pictures' *Wake Island*, made in 1942.

Sgt. William Hamilton (*left*) and Lt. John Kinney performed miracles of improvisation in keeping the Wildcats flying.

(Above) Marine Staff Sergeant Charles Holmes of Bonham, Texas, strolls down a Honolulu street in November, 1941, just prior to being shipped out to Wake Island. Two other men of the 1st Defense Battalion, Corporal Frank Gross *(top left)* of Independence, Missouri, and Corporal Jess Nowlin of Richardson, Texas, are seen in photos taken after the war (Nowlin's picture was taken in October, 1945, upon his release from Oak Knoll Hospital in San Francisco).

The motion picture *Wake Island* brought home to Americans the violence and suffering endured by the real-life marines, sailors, soldiers, and civilians trapped on the atoll during the 16-day siege.

A just-returned Japanese fighter pilot *(top)* tells his comrades how he shot down a U.S. plane. Aerial view of civilian barracks on Peale Island *(bottom)* was taken from an attacking bomber. Photos are from a Japanese picture book.

Chapter Four

The Second Round

TUESDAY, DECEMBER 9, began bright and clear. All hands were at general quarters for the dawn alert, guns manned, ammunition ready, as the morning patrol searched sky and sea around the island. There was no sign of the enemy.

The men were bleary-eyed from work, from lack of sleep, but there was hot coffee with morning chow. That is more important than it may sound. Perhaps you cannot know how important it can be until you cannot get it. There are times in war when hot coffee is almost plasma for the spirit. As they drank steaming coffee that second morning of the war, men sagging with weariness made wisecracks about the Japs.

The work went on. All over the island men were digging in. Getting underground was an intensely personal problem. Now and then they looked with tired eyes to see if the bombers were coming back, before they had a hole to hide in.

At the airfield, Lieutenant Kinney and Sergeant Hamilton reported that they had four planes able to fly, though one of them lacked an auxiliary fuel tank.

Civilian crews with bulldozers were building bomb-proof dugouts for the surviving personnel at the airfield. Bomb shelters were also being constructed at battery positions, along the shore southeastward from Camp

One and in the civilian area around Camp Two.

We could have made good use of every man on the island in working parties, but I ordered that at least one gun in each battery should be kept fully manned at all times. When there was no alert, the rest of the gun crews turned to on the never-ending task of improving the battery positions. On Wilkes, for instance, a detail was at work that morning filling five hundred sandbags and placing them for battery protection. On Peale, civilians were filling sandbags and a Marine was hauling them to Godbold's battery in a truck and trailer.

Some of the gunners were beefing because the Jap bombers had come in too low for effective 3-inch fire. There was a lot of argument whether the enemy would come in low next time or go upstairs. It seemed logical to assume the Japs would come in low again because then the 3-inch would be least effective. But Lieutenant Lewis predicted flatly that the Japs would come in high. Our fire had been ineffective the first day, but we had thrown up a lot of it, and Lewis argued that would make them climb. He reasoned that while the Japs would not be as safe higher up, they would feel safer. He should have made book on it because he was right.

The Japs came at 11:45. There were twenty-seven. Again they were twin-tailed, two-motored, heavy Navy bombers—land-based planes from Roi. Again they knew what they wanted and where to find it.

But this time we hit them first. Lieutenant Kliewer and Sergeant Hamilton were flying the midday patrol. They intercepted the enemy well south of Wake at eleven thousand feet. They attacked at once, two against twenty-seven. They struck at the wings of the Japanese squadron, trying to break the formation before the enemy reached the island. That would make the bombing more haphazard. It would also make the big bombers easier to kill.

The squadron held its course as the Wildcats slashed at its flanks. The Jap gunners tried to fight them off, but

Kliewer and Hamilton attacked again and again. Now one of the bombers was wobbling out of formation. He was badly hit. The pilot fought to keep his plane in place, but the Wildcats dived on him. They shot him into flames. The burning Jap spun down into the sea. It was our first blood of the battle.

The Wildcats attacked again, but two planes were not enough to stop twenty-seven. The rest of the bombers held the course. We could see them now. They were coming in above eight thousand feet. This time the 3-inch batteries had a chance of hitting back. They were firing before the Japs crossed the bomb release line, and one of the Japs began trailing smoke as they came over the island.

The Japs were passing across Peacock Point, heading toward Camp Two. They were high up, but there was nothing myopic about their bombing. They laid a line of bombs across the Point.

The 5-inch guns were not anti-aircraft weapons, so Barninger's men could only crouch helpless in their holes as the first bombs came crashing down into the middle of their position. Concussion dazed them. The detonations pelted them with dirt and debris. Private John Katchak did not have time to know that a bomb exploded on the edge of his foxhole.

The Japs were over the battery now. When a bomber is directly above you, you are safe from its load. The bombs dropped then will fall beyond you. Sometimes that is hard to remember. As Pfc Mike Olenowski said, "All you know is that they look like they're coming right at you." Now as the bombers passed over them, shaken men looked from the blasted position as though they could not understand that they were still alive.

I was standing near my CP, watching the attack. The explosions were at the airfield now, but this time the bombs fell along the north side of the strip. Major Putnam had nothing there for them to hit.

A gasoline truck was being driven to cover, zig-zagging

into the brush in the driver's frantic effort to dodge the bombs. He would have made it, we could tell afterward, but he guessed wrong when he made the last turn. He ran right into the bombers' path, and a direct hit destroyed the truck. Three Marines were in it. We did not find them for ten days.

Another Jap was in trouble now. He was smoking badly, wobbling. We could see the bombers were almost over Camp Two. A communications man said, "Them poor bastards." Nobody else said anything, but we were all thinking of the wounded in the hospital.

The hospital was a one-story, T-shaped building, containing a couple of wards, several private rooms, an operating room and a clinic. There the sick and wounded lay waiting. That was all most of them could do. They'd heard the sound of the first bombs, dulled by distance, and then lay listening to the explosions coming toward them across the island. Then they heard the sickening whistle of bombs coming down. They were the target. The enemy let the bottoms drop out of his bombracks.

The explosions at Camp Two came too close together for us to count. And the Japs were strafing, slashing the camp with blasts of bullets. Bombs hit a warehouse and the metal shop. The Navy radio station was destroyed. Buildings and equipment were smashed or left burning.

The hospital was hit. Most of the sick and wounded were killed. Some still alive in the wreckage had been freshly wounded. The enemy droned on as men stumbled from holes to help the wounded.

The Japs made a pass at Peale Island, too, pounding the hotel and such targets as had escaped destruction the first day, and then they headed home, but this time they paid for their fun. Lewis' battery on Peacock Point, Godbold's on Peale and the .50's had thrown furious fire against the attack. Godbold's battery alone fired a hundred rounds in its brief minutes of action. And the Marines' aim was good. Our batteries had five of the Japs smoking as they left the island. They were still in sight when one of the wounded bombers exploded in the air. The other damaged Japs were smoking so badly that our aviation men calculated they would never get home. A Japanese journal captured at the end of the war indicates that 14 of the bombers were damaged by antiaircraft fire during this attack.

I made an inspection after the raid, as I usually did after an attack, as much for morale as anything else. The men knew that a commanding officer's post in battle is usually at the CP, directing and coordinating the activities of the various units, but they like to see him around from time to time. It is a bad thing for an outfit in combat when men begin to feel they have been stuck off somewhere and forgotten.

One heard Marines, exhausted as they were, making jokes about the raid. They'd had their chance to hit back at the enemy, and they liked the feel of it. It was a lot better than the first day, when we'd had to take a licking lying down.

We'd been hard hit, though. Our worst casualties were at the hospital. Twenty-one patients were killed there— Marines, sailors and civilians. Eleven of the patients killed were Marines who had been wounded in the first day's attack on the airfield. Of Major Putnam's squadron of sixty-one officers and men, twenty-three were now dead and a dozen wounded.

Among the survivors at the hospital was the battered, crippled, but apparently indestructible Master Technical Sergeant Paszkiewicz. By all the laws of probability, he should have been killed at the airport in the first attack and at the hospital in the second, but all he needed was a little more patching. As he lay there, getting patched up again, Sergeant Paszkiewicz commented on the ancestry and morals of the Japanese pungently, at length and with an amazing lack of repetition. Somebody said he'd bet the Japs couldn't shut up the durable sergeant with anything less than a direct hit.

At least fifty civilian casualties were reported from Camp Two, mostly wounded, many with only minor injuries, but I believe the report involved considerable duplication.

On Peale Island, five wounded civilians stumbled into the gun positions. They had been filling sandbags when the Japs attacked. They were treated by a corpsman and sent by truck to the wrecked hospital.

Corporal K.L. Marvin returned to Godbold's battery with the truck in which he had been hauling sandbags filled by the civilians. He was wounded on the head, but was more concerned with his fervent hope that he might never again have to nursemaid a truck through a bombing. He had found the experience decidedly unpleasant, even though he had succeeded in saving the truck despite a Jap's attempt to bag it. After being treated by a corpsman, Corporal Marvin returned to his gun. It apparently did not occur to the corporal that he could have abandoned the truck to destruction instead of risking his skin to save it.

Trucks and all other equipment were precious on Wake. Our losses of equipment were especially serious because almost none of it could be replaced. For example: The bombs dropped in Barninger's position on Peacock Point that day had riddled the range-finder tube with flying fragments and shattered one of the lenses. The instrument was damaged beyond repair. So from that time on, Barninger's 5-inch guns had to be operated without a range-finder.

Most serious of the material losses that day, however, was the destruction of the Navy radio station. Pan-American's radio station had been destroyed the previous day. Now our best means of communication with the outside world was the Army radio truck. The truck, now of priceless value to us, had been near the airfield at first. Then it was moved into the brush east of the airfield for greater safety. Later, as a final precaution, Commander Cunningham had the radio equipment transferred from the truck to an empty powder magazine.

We also began shifting ammunition to clear two of the larger magazines for use as a hospital. We divided the hospital instead of trying to house it in a single dugout, not only to provide more room but as a precaution against losing both our doctors by a single bomb hit.

There were four of these large magazines. Beginning at the southeastern corner of the airfield, they were spaced out in a line along the road to Camp Two. The new hospital was divided between the magazines at either extremity of this line. The magazines were perhaps forty-by-twenty-feet in size, with fifteen-foot ceilings. They were built of reinforced concrete and were half-sunken in the ground, with dirt piled on top. This is called "elephant back" construction because that is what the finished structure resembles from the outside. There were supposed to be more magazines on the island, on Wilkes as well as Wake, but the Japanese attacked before the program was advanced very far beyond these four.

The transfer of the hospital to the two magazines was not completed until that night. Small generators provided both magazines with electric power. As lights in the magazines did not endanger the island blackout, they could be kept lit at night.

Meanwhile, through the afternoon and deep into the night, work went on, work that had been interrupted by the attack, work to repair damage done by the attack, work to get ready for the next attack.

One of Lieutenant Lewis' 3-inch AA guns had been damaged in the attack on Peacock Point, so I directed Marine Gunner C.B. McKinstry to move the damaged gun to Wilkes Island and bring back one of the guns from the unmanned 3-inch battery there.

That night, as soon as darkness gave concealment for the work, I moved Lieutenant Lewis' battery to a new position a little over five hundred yards farther in from Peacock Point. Since my return to the States, I have heard some criticism of this move, and so I feel I should discuss it here in some detail.

In theory, you should place your anti-aircraft guns where they can reach out as far as possible and engage an enemy before he reaches the bomb release line. This theory governed the selection of Lewis' original position on Peacock Point, and it is true that from the new position he could not reach out so far with his fire in the direction from which the enemy usually attacked.

However, on Wake, I was faced with more than a purely theoretical problem. I was convinced that the enemy had spotted Lewis' position. Not only had they damaged one of his guns, but a Jap plane broke formation during the raid and circled over the position, apparently taking aerial photographs to guide the bombers in the next attack. I felt sure that next time the enemy would come after Lewis' guns.

In making my decision to move the battery, I was influenced by an incident of the battle of Crete which Lord Louis Mountbatten had related at Pearl Harbor and which I had heard from Colonel Bone. It seems that when the Germans attacked Crete, one British battery had a position which was in every way ideal, theoretically perfect. So the battery commander did not move his guns to a secondary position even after the Germans spotted his battery. The result was that the Germans methodically set about destroying the position, finally dropping paratroops under cover of a smoke screen. The experience convinced the battery commander that, if he could have done it all over, he would have kept his guns as mobile as possible even though that would have meant abandoning what seemed to be theoretically the best possible position.

On Wake, if we had had sufficient local protection it is probable that I should not have moved Lewis' guns. But we did not have such local protection nor were our batteries able to give each other such closely interlocking support fire. I moved Lewis because I felt certain the enemy had spotted his position. My primary purpose was to keep the batteries in action, and I knew there could be no replacements if they were knocked out. Unless I could keep them in action, the enemy would be able to bomb at will until he levelled the island. In the light of what happened next day, I am convinced I was correct in shifting Lewis' guns to the new position.

My orders were that Lewis should begin the move as soon as it was dark; that he should leave two guns in position until the other two were set up in the new position and ready to fire. While I did not expect a night bombing attack, we were taking no chances of being caught off base by a surprise raid.

Moving the guns, each weighing eight tons, was a long and difficult task in the darkness. The outrigger legs of the 3-inch AA guns folded to form the body and then the guns were made mobile by mounting them on "bogies," removable trucks consisting of an axle with two big pneumatic-tired wheels. Each gun had to be jacked up so the bogie could be rolled under it and then the gun was lowered onto the bogie, made fast and hauled to the new position. That was only part of the job. Sandbags had to be filled and put in place at the new position. Ammunition had to be hauled by truck and scattered in dumps of a hundred rounds each within easy handling distance of the guns. The position had to be camouflaged. It was five o'clock the next morning, December 10, before the battery was set up in its new position and ready to fire.

At the old position, dummy guns constructed from timber were placed where Lewis' guns had been so that the position would seem unchanged when viewed from the air.

That morning I sent Gunner McKinstry to take command of the crewless 3-inch AA battery on Wilkes. Aided by a single Marine, McKinstry manned the battery by forming bluejackets from the searchlight detail and civilian volunteers into scratch gun crews. The battery had no fire control equipment and the 3-inch guns did not have sights, so they were useless except for short-range or point-blank fire. Consequently, Gunner McKinstry set up the battery for beach defense in case the enemy tried a landing on Wilkes.

About 10:45, the enemy attacked. Eighteen bombers this time. They were higher still today, coming in at eighteen thousand feet. Our four remaining planes were up to meet them.

The Jap formation divided for the attack. Nine bombers headed straight for Lewis' old position. We had been right in guessing they had spotted the position, that they would throw a Sunday punch in an effort to wipe out the battery. As Lieutenant Barninger put it, "The Japs rolled right down the alley that had Lewis' old position for its Number One pin." They pounded the area with bombs, scoring direct hits on two of the dummy guns and near misses beside the others. Lieutenant Lewis reported that his battery would have been knocked out of action if he had been in his original position.

The enemy struck heavily at Wilkes Island. Both 5-inch guns in the Wilkes battery were badly damaged. All the ready ammunition was blown up. A direct hit on a storage shed set off 125 tons of dynamite. The tremendous explosion flattened everything in the area. The blast destroyed all concealment in the area, knocked out one of the 3-inch guns and wrecked the searchlight truck half a mile away. One of the searchlights was blown over and so badly damaged that it never functioned properly again.

Nine of the bombers hit Peale island. As the enemy attacked, the power plant of Godbold's battery failed because of a defective carburetor. Power is necessary for the calculating mechanism which enables AA gunners to place their shells at the spot in the air where, theoretically, the plane will be when the shell arrives. Lacking power, the guns have to be fired by local control, which is hit-or-miss, so Godbold could not expect effective results. He threw up enough flak, however, to keep the enemy too high for accuracy and his gunners got one Jap. The Jap was smoking thickly as the enemy ended his first run and that Jap did not come back for the second pass at

Peale. The second run by eight bombers was as ineffective as the first. All the bombs dropped over Peale Island that day fell into the lagoon or on the reef off Toki Point.

Meanwhile, our four Grummans attacked the Jap formations repeatedly. Captain Henry Elrod knocked down two of the big bombers before the enemy turned tail for home. A Marine watching the fury of Elrod's attack exclaimed, "Hammering Hank is sure giving 'em hell!" The name stuck. From then on, Elrod was "Hammering Hank."

Considering the force of the enemy's blows at Wilkes Island and Peacock Point, our casualties were surprisingly light. On Peacock, two Marines were wounded when a bomb exploded beside a machine gun pit. On Wilkes, Corporal Tokryman was killed, two Marines and a civilian wounded.

As the enemy departed, we began repairing bomb damage and strengthening positions. On Peale, Godbold's battery repaired their power plant and obtained a small Diesel generator set from Camp Two. They used the Diesel to provide the battery with power and kept the regular power plant as a reserve unit.

On Wilkes, Gunner McKinstry moved his three remaining 3-inch guns to a position nearer the shore. He camouflaged the position with burned brush, but he lacked sandbags to give protection to his crews of volunteers.

On Wake itself, we set up new dummy guns at Lewis' original position on Peacock Point. That night Lewis moved three of his guns to a new position where he remained for the rest of the battle. This final position was at the toe of the horseshoe, on the lagoon side. We selected this position because in order to hit it, the enemy would be forced to make a run at the battery alone, with the chances that most of the bombs would fall into the lagoon. Lewis had no crew for his fourth gun, so this weapon was set up on the west shore to be manned for beach defense if the enemy attempted a landing. During the night, I moved my CP to one of the dugouts constructed along the beach to the east of Camp One.

The most serious damage from the attack that day was sustained by the 5-inch battery on Wilkes Island. Second Lieutenant J.A. McAlister checked the damage and reported range-finder, time-interval apparatus, Navy plotting board, the phones at both guns—all damaged beyond repair. The pointer and trainer scope of his Gun No. 1 and the elevation receiver were damaged beyond repair and the firing lock and training rack were damaged. The trainer scope of his Gun No. 2 was damaged beyond repair and the firing lock was damaged.

Lieutenant McAlister was able to get two trainer scopes from our small stock of spare parts. He replaced the trainer scope on Gun No. 2 and put the other trainer scope on the pointer scope bracket of Gun No. 1. He made such other repairs as he could, but much of the damaged fire control equipment was beyond replacement or improvisation. The battery simply had to do without it. It was perhaps just as well for our peace of mind that we didn't know that before that morning we would have to depend on our 5-inch batteries to meet an attack by a Japanese task force.

Lessons were being rapidly learned, however. As Major Putnam commented later, "The original raid...was tactically well conceived and skillfully executed, but thereafter their tactics were stupid, and the best that can be said of their skill is that they had excellent flight discipline. The hour and altitude of their arrival over the island was almost constant and their method of attack invariable, so that it was a simple matter to meet them, and they never after that first day got through unopposed."

Our antiaircraft fire was driving the Jap bombers higher and higher on each successive raid. This contributed toward less accurate bombing as one attack followed another.

Chapter Five

Task Force

I WAS ASLEEP IN THE CP dugout when the first phone call came. A lookout reported seeing "movement" in the darkness offshore to the south. I glanced at my watch. It was not yet three o'clock in the morning of December 11.

"What kind of movement?"

"Just something seemed to be moving. Then we couldn't see it any more."

Perhaps there had been a faint blink of light, too. The lookout couldn't be sure. All he knew was that he had seen a movement at sea south of the island.

Corporal Robert McC. Brown was on the telephone watch at the CP. I told him to check all posts by phone. Meanwhile, I considered the chances. I did not want to break out my weary men for a false alarm. They needed rest too badly. But neither did I want the enemy to catch us off balance. The question I had to answer to myself in the next few minutes was, "What had the lookout seen?" Perhaps it was only his imagination. Strain can make a man imagine things in the dark. Perhaps he had caught a glimpse of an American submarine surfaced in the protecting dark to recharge batteries. We knew a couple of our submarines were somewhere near Wake. One had sent a sick man ashore to our hospital just before hostilities began. Or perhaps it *was* the enemy. Perhaps the Japs thought we had been softened enough by bombing to be taken. These were alternatives I tried to weigh as Corporal Brown checked the posts around the island. It seemed like a long time, but it took only a few minutes.

He looked up from the phone. A post near the boat channel had seen "some sort of movement."

"Did they see any lights?"

He queried. Then, "No, sir, no lights. Whatever it was, was quite a ways off."

Then Captain Platt called from Wilkes, "It sure looks like there are some ships out there."

I told my runner to come along. We walked down to the beach near the boat channel. I studied the sea through the night glasses, powerful binoculars with a wide field of vision. If anything had come close to shore, it had moved out again. The sea seemed empty. But then—

"Well," I said, "there they are."

They were away on the horizon, hardly more than blurs a little darker than the surrounding darkness, but through the night glasses there was no mistaking them. They were ships—and we knew there was no American task force anywhere near Wake Island.

We walked back to the CP and I passed the word to prepare for battle. My order to all hands was:

"Hold your fire until I give the word."

We could not tell exactly the strength of the enemy at that distance in the dark, but the force seemed large enough for me to feel sure they would have vessels that could outgun anything we had. It seemed to me that our one slim chance was to draw in the enemy close enough for our 5-inch guns to hit him crippling blows at the start of the attack.

I phoned Commander Cunningham that ships were standing in.

"Are you sure?"

"I've seen them myself."

"I'll be over."

I called Major Putnam at the airfield: How many

planes did he have in commission?

Four.

When would it be light enough to send them up?

About half an hour before daylight. That was the earliest they could be expected to attack effectively.

"Don't take off until I open fire," I said. "I'm trying to draw them in, and the planes would give the show away."

"Okay," he said. "Good luck."

I wondered how many planes the Japs would send to cover the landing and what our four Grummans could do against them. Well, we'd see.

I went outside, taking along an extension phone, and stood by the dugout to observe the enemy. Commander Cunningham drove down to see the approaching ships and then returned to his CP after I informed him that all positions were ready for action.

It was a little lighter. The enemy was still well off the island, coming in from the south, but he was closing fast. With the glasses, I counted three light cruisers, six destroyers, two transports and four smaller vessels, probably gunboats. Some observers reported several additional vessels, cruisers and destroyers. Information developed after the war from Japanese sources shows that the smaller total is accurate. In any event, it was all the Japs needed. It was more than enough to take Wake Island. The Jap cruisers had at least 6-inch guns to oppose our 5-inch batteries. That meant simply that they could stand off safely beyond our fire until they had pounded us to pulp. Then they could send in those two transport-loads of fresh troops to make the landing against what scraps of our force remained.

As I watched them closing in, I cautioned the batteries again, "Under no circumstances fire until I give the word."

A cruiser was leading the Japs in, well in advance of the rest of the flotilla. The main force was still twelve thousand yards off the island, heading toward the beach, when the leading cruiser swung broadside off Peacock Point, out perhaps eight thousand yards, and started a new course parallel to the island. She opened fire. It was five o'clock in the morning.

The Jap cruiser steamed the length of the island, still firing, and then reversed her run. She steamed leisurely back and forth, bombarding us, and each run brought the cruiser closer in to shore. Off beyond, I could see the rest of the Japanese force closing in.

On Peacock Point, Lieutenant Barninger removed his camouflage. He guessed—correctly—that the higher ground behind the battery would prevent his guns from being spotted in the dim light. His guns began to track the cruiser, but the Jap didn't suspect he was there. Not a single shell fell near Barninger's position.

A few minutes later the other two cruisers opened fire at area targets along the south shore of the island from Peacock Point to the vicinity of Camp One. The high velocity 6-inch shells set fire to the diesel oil tanks between Camp One and Wilkes Channel, but otherwise the shellfire was ineffective.

I do not want to give the impression that we were being subjected to a holocaust of fire. The Jap was apparently just trying to find out what we had, firing to make us open up if we had anything left.

The cruiser was now seven thousand yards off. Three destroyers moved swiftly ahead of the approaching column and began firing as they closed. Meanwhile the remaining Japanese ships proceeded behind the cruiser and destroyer screen to take stations for their various missions. We had not fired a single shot. It was a calculated risk that the enemy would think the bombings had knocked out our guns.

Shells continued dropping all along the beach on Wake and Wilkes. Riflemen and machine gunners hugged their holes. Their fight would come when the Japs tried to come ashore. Their job until then was to keep themselves alive.

At the guns, men grumbled because the order did not come to fire. Or they stood in tight silence, waiting, as the enemy searched for them with exploding shells.

The CP phone kept ringing. Barninger and McAlister were begging for permission to open fire. Corporal Brown kept relaying the same reply:

"Hold your fire till the Major gives the word."

It was rather close figuring, and we would not have a second chance. We had six 5-inch guns, but the Peale Island battery could not bear on the course the Japs were coming. Only Barninger's two guns on Peacock Point and McAlister's pair on Wilkes could be brought to bear. Both batteries were partly crippled by lack of fire control equipment destroyed by the bombing. Barninger lacked a rangefinder. McAlister had to guess both range and deflection. And the enemy was coming in for the kill. The nearest Jap cruiser was now less than five thousand yards offshore, still shelling the island.

A Marine said, though naturally not to me, "What does that dumb little blankety-blank want us to do? Let 'em run over us without even spitting back?"

It must have looked that way. The enemy was right in our front yard. The nearest Jap, the cruiser, was only forty-five hundred yards from Barninger's position. The time was 6:10. I gave the order, "Commence firing!"

Barninger took the cruiser that was almost sitting in his lap and McAlister's guns fired at the leading destroyer, perhaps seven thousand yards away.

Barninger's first salvo was over. The cruiser tried to run for it, a zig-zagging race to escape from the trap we'd sprung. If she could get out of range, she could lie in safety while pounding us with her heavier guns.

Barninger, directing fire from the roof of his CP, lowered the range five hundred yards. The flash of his first salvo had betrayed his position. Now the cruiser was returning fire as she fled. Shell fragments struck the hut on top of which he was standing, but he escaped unhit.

The battery's fire was straddling the cruiser. Barninger corrected range. Short that time. Try again. Another straddle. Try again. At fifty-seven hundred yards, he caught her. Both shells of the salvo crashed into the cruiser's side just above the waterline. Smoke and steam gushed from the holes. She lost speed, but still tried to limp away.

At seven thousand yards, she was hit twice more in almost the same place—close to the waterline, a little a-baft of midships. She veered crazily. The smoke and steam poured more thickly from her side. The crippled ship tried vainly to turn into the smoke, to hide in the cloud spilled from her own wounds.

A destroyer tried to save her by racing in to lay a smoke screen between the cruiser and the shore. A shell exploded on the destroyer's fo-c'sle. Barninger reported the shell that hit the destroyer was "just a lucky shot that missed the cruiser." But the Jap destroyer turned tail, abandoning the battered cruiser.

Barninger's gunners got one more hit before the cruiser dragged herself out of range. The shell struck the forward turret, silencing the guns.

A slight delay in Battery L's commencement of fire resulted from Lt. McAlister's attempt to refine the rough firing data which he obtained without a range finder which had been blown out of operation by the explosion of the Wilkes Island dynamite cache on December 10th. Once in action, however, he engaged a succession of enemy ships with excellent results. The targets which seemed to fill the battery's field of fire consisted of a division of three destroyers, both transports and two of the three cruisers. He guessed range and deflection well enough to hit the leading destroyer with his third salvo at forty-five hundred yards. The ship literally blew up. In less than two minutes, it had vanished with all hands. Recently I have learned that this destroyer was the *Hayate* and that she was the first Japanese surface craft to be sunk during the war by United States forces.

The gunners let out a yell when the destroyer exploded.

They stood cheering instead of shifting fire to the next destroyer. They were jolted back to their senses by a bellow from an old China Marine, Platoon Sergeant Henry Bedell:

"Knock it off, you bastards, and get back on the guns! What d'y' think this is, a ball game?"

He was a thin, dried-looking man, not large, but he had a voice that would have shamed a clap of thunder. The gunners snapped to it as though booted in the pants. Somebody cracked, "No wonder the Japs took off—they thought Bedell was yelling at them." But that was later. Just then nobody had time to make wisecracks. They were throwing shells too fast.

McAlister quickly shifted his fire to the destroyer which had been following the *Hayate*. She was by now so close to shore that I was forced to restrain several overeager .30 machine gunners from opening fire. One hit by the 5-inch guns was observed before the troublesome onshore wind blanketed the target with smoke. When last seen the destroyer had turned tail and was beating a retreat to seaward. Firing continued into the smoke, but results could not be observed. McAlister now checked fire on the retreating destroyer and trained his sights on the leader of the two transports which were steaming to his south at about 10,000 yards offshore. After being hit once, she too turned to seaward and retired behind the heavy smoke screen.

McAlister's guns were out of ammunition. The gunners had to suspend fire to lug a fresh supply from the magazines. But after that, civilian volunteers took over the ammunition detail, freeing the Marines to keep up fire as long as they had a target.

A cruiser was now picked up steaming northward off the west end of Wilkes at a range of 9,000 yards. She was taken under fire and was hit aft. After a few salvos she too displayed her distaste for Marine gunfire by turning tail and fleeing to seaward. She appeared to be on fire.

The Japs were in panic, zig-zagging wildly to escape. Destroyers raced frantically about, trying to screen the larger ships with smoke, trying to spread smoke to cover their own escape. The enemy's movement to the northwest of Kuku Point brought them under fire from the 5-inch battery on Peale Island.

The enemy was on the run, but he was blasting with all he could bring to bear, trying to cover the flight. From Peale, Lieutenant Kessler reported "heavy shell-fire received in the battery position."

No targets now remained within range of Battery L. In one hour's hot work they had fired 60 salvos (120 rounds) and had sunk one destroyer and damaged another; they had also damaged a cruiser and a transport. Two of McAlister's men had sustained slight wounds which were dressed by hospital corpsmen on Wilkes Island.

On Peale, the gunners hit a destroyer and saw her stern burst into flames. Gun No. 2 was put out of action when the recoil-cylinder filling-pipe plug blew out. The flying steel plug hit Corporal A.F. Terry in the side. He staggered and stood gasping, but wouldn't wait for first aid. He stumbled with the rest of the crew to serve Gun No. 1 as ammunition handlers, so this remaining gun would not have to break fire.

Muzzle blast knocked out the range finder. Shellfire landing in the position cut the communication lines between the battery CP and the gun. They had to fire by local control. But observers reported Sergeant Alton J. Bertels' crew got at least one hit on a destroyer before the enemy was out of range. (Sgt. Bertels died of tuberculosis while in prison camp.)

On Wilkes, observing through binoculars, Gunner McKinstry saw a transport that had fled McAlister's fire. She was badly hit, lying dead in the water. A destroyer came alongside and took off at least some of the Jap troops. They may not have had time to get them all. For just as the destroyer pulled hastily away, the transport exploded and sank.

I do not know whether this was the transport McAlister hit at ten thousand yards. He last saw her disappearing into a smoke screen.

The Japanese force was now in full retirement. Their plans had been thwarted by unfavorable weather, but more importantly by the stout and accurate fire from the beach. They steamed away over the horizon, to Kwajalein, as we later learned, to regroup, refit, and prepare for another try.

The time was 7:10. I ordered, "Cease firing."

This was exactly the right moment for an air attack to harry the retreating Japanese.

Our four Grummans had taken off when I gave the word that we had engaged the enemy. When they found there was no enemy aircraft, a fact which surprised us all, the Grummans joined the attack on the task force, pounding it home with bombing and strafing long after the enemy fled beyond range of our guns.

The method improvised by Captain Freuler for hooking bombs on the Grummans enabled our planes to attack the enemy with something more than strafing fire, but the planes could carry only two 100-pound bombs at a time. So they had to shuttle back and forth, rearming after each attack, seeking out the scattered enemy, diving through flak to lay the bombs right in his lap. Then back to the field, with a few more flak holes in the plane, to hook on another pair of bombs. And out again to bomb and strafe beyond the horizon. All we ashore could see of that last chapter of our victory was, from time to time, the smoke from an explosion miles out to sea.

Elrod and Tharin surprised the Japs while they were transferring survivors from a crippled cruiser, apparently Barninger's victim. They dived to attack, holding their bombs until they couldn't miss. It was low-level bombing with a vengeance—"smokestack bombing," somebody called it—and it killed the cruiser. She was sink-ing as they swung away to strafe the fleeing rescue vessel.

It is possible this was the same cruiser which Lieutenant Kinney sighted burning twenty miles south of the island. When he returned to the field, he made his report with the injured air of a man who has just drawn his fourth ace when the game is raided:

"As I prepared to bomb this ship, it blew up and sank."

Freuler caught a transport. In their panic to get away the Japanese war vessels apparently had run off and left the slower transport to shift for herself. Now Freuler came in low and laid a bomb smack on her stern. She was still underway, however, when last seen—and Freuler had to come home, beating his gums because he didn't have another bomb.

Each time the Grummans attacked, almost hedgehopping to increase their chances of a hit, they had to wade through flying flak. All the planes were hit. Captain Freuler's oil line was shot away. He had bullet holes through a cylinder and the air cooler. I still don't see how he managed to make the field, but he did, with a beautiful dead-stick landing. His engine was a total loss.

Elrod's plane was shot-up even worse. We watched him trying to reach the island. We could see the plane was in serious trouble, wobbling badly, losing altitude all the time as though it were being dragged down. It seemed certain he would never make the island. But he did, by a slight margin of a few feet, and crash-landed on the beach.

Putnam and I were among those who hurried down to pull what was left of Hammering Hank Elrod out of the wreck. He climbed out unhurt, but he wasn't thinking about the miracle of his escape. His plane was a total loss and he couldn't think of anything else. His first words to us were an apology for failing to bring his plane safely home, and he kept on apologizing for it, over and over, as though it had been his fault. He made only passing reference to the death blow he'd dealt an enemy cruiser. What he wanted us to understand was, "Honest, I'm sorry as hell about the plane."

In addition to our own artillery fire and aircraft we had, though we did not know it until later, the assistance of the U.S. Submarine *Triton* (Lieutenant Commander W.A. Lent). She fired on at least one Jap ship.

We now had only two planes able to fly, but that was the most serious result of the Japanese task force's attempt to take the island. The enemy had thrown a lot of shellfire at us, but the only serious damage was the destruction of the Diesel fuel tank.

Trying to add up the enemy's losses, we found it difficult to decide just which ships should be credited to our shore batteries and which to the planes. We decided that the transport which had been seen to explode and sink probably had been bagged by a submarine after being hit by our fire. Recently, however, I learned that the submarine *Triton* did not receive credit for a kill.

Not that it really mattered. What mattered was this—our shore batteries, our planes and the submarine, as a team, had smashed a Japanese task force that should have wiped us out with ease.

The best estimate we could make then of the enemy's losses was one light cruiser, two destroyers, one gunboat and one transport sunk, with the loss of two or three thousand Jap lives.

Other estimates of losses which have come to my attention recently vary widely. A Japanese officer interrogated after the war stated that we sank nine ships and killed 5,350 men. It was determined by our Naval historians from the study of captured documents and interrogation that we did not sink a cruiser as we thought we had. All three cruisers which participated in the December 11th attempt returned on December 23rd. Also, the Navy estimate of Jap casualties published in official documents is much lower. They place the enemy casualties at 700, mostly dead. The accurate figure will never be known. The important fact is that we had beaten off an attack of a vastly larger force than our own and that we had inflicted heavy losses. We had four casualties, a corporal with a bruised side and three men with minor scratches.

As Corporal Brown observed: "It's been quite a day, Major, hasn't it?"

But the day wasn't over.

A little before ten o'clock that morning, a squadron of Jap bombers attacked. We had only two Grummans able to fly, piloted by Lieutenants Davidson and Kinney. They attacked, two against eighteen. Lieutenant Davidson shot down two of the big bombers. Lieutenant Kinney was credited with a probable. Our AA batteries shot down one bomber and had three others trailing thick smoke as they turned tail for home. That added up to a bag of three bombers, another probable and three more we didn't think could get home. All they hurt was empty sand.

It remained, however, for Second Lieutenant Kliewer to top-off our day of victory and put pink icing on the cake.

I never tried to keep up with the gossip of junior officers, but I heard enough to know that Lieutenant Kliewer, a tall, thin and rather reserved young man, was supposed to have a serious personal problem. They said he came of a deeply religious family which was gravely concerned when he joined the Corps because the taking of human life, under any circumstances, was contrary to their faith. His problem, then, was what he would do if his faith and his duty conflicted. They said he still couldn't answer the question whether he could personally kill anybody or not. At least, that was the story among the junior officers.

That afternoon, when it was time for the evening patrol to take off, Lieutenant Kliewer's plane wouldn't start. It took fifteen minutes to get it going, so he was alone when he took off. Lieutenant Kliewer was not the sort of man who discussed his private feelings, so I do not know what he thought or what questions he may have asked himself as he flew alone over miles of empty sea. All any of us know about that patrol is the official report:

Twenty-five miles off the island, bearing 225 degrees from Wake, Lieutenant Kliewer sighted something below him. It looked very small from ten thousand feet. It was a submarine completely surfaced.

Maneuvering to come at the submarine out of the sun so the crew would not spot him, Kliewer went into a fast dive to get near enough to identify the sub. As he neared her, plummeting down, he saw what she was: a Jap. He fired. He sprayed bullets at the broadside of the sub until he had to pull out of his dive or crash. He made a right 90-degree turn and attacked again.

He had only two chances to hit the narrow target with a bomb. So he didn't let them go until he was so low that shrapnel flying up from his own bombs tore large holes in his wing and tail sections.

The bombs missed the submarine, but both exploded within fifteen feet of her. She was hurt, but how badly he didn't know. He attacked again, strafing the Jap until his guns were empty, and then he flew home to report.

Major Putnam took off at once to finish off the damaged sub if he could find her. At the spot where Kliewer last saw the submarine Putnam found a large oil slick that could mean only one thing: "Credit Kliewer with one Jap sub."

Navy studies made after the war developed a picture of the December 11th landing attempt from the Japanese side. The reduction of Wake as well as Guam, Makin and Tarawa was assigned by war plans to Admiral Inouye, commander of the Japanese Fourth Fleet based on Truk. Guam, Makin and Tarawa were taken by December 10th. The Japs knew that the development of our defenses on Wake was much farther along, and they estimated that we had 1,000 troops and 600 civilian laborers on the

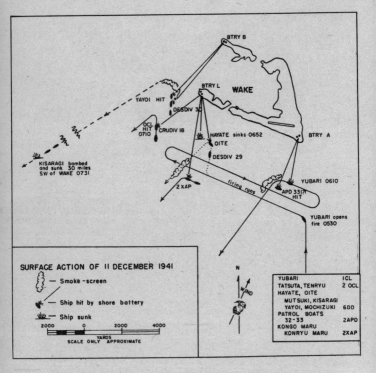

SURFACE ACTION OF 11 DECEMBER 1941

— Smoke-screen

— Ship hit by shore battery

— Ship sunk

YUBARI		1CL
TATSUTA, TENRYU		2 OCL
HAYATE, OITE		
MUTSUKI, KISARAGI		
YAYOI, MOCHIZUKI		6DD
PATROL BOATS		
32·33		2APD
KONGO MARU		
KONRYU MARU		2XAP

island. The preliminary air operations, including the necessary aerial softening, was assigned to the Commander of the Twenty-Fourth Air Flotilla. His plan was orthodox, but not particularly imaginative. His first attack was an effort to cripple our fighter aircraft; his second was essentially a mop-up for the first. The Twenty-Fourth Air Flotilla next settled down to methodically knocking out our antiaircraft and seacoast batteries.

The conduct of the amphibious assault was assigned to Rear Admiral Kajioka, Commander Destroyer Squadron 6, who flew his flag in the new light cruiser *Yubari*. His plan was to land 150 men on Wilkes Island and 300 men on the south side of Wake with the initial mission of capturing the airfield. He did not consider the north shore or Peale Island suitable for landings.

The task force at his disposal for the operation consisted of one light cruiser, two obsolescent light cruisers, six destroyers, two destroyer transports, two new transports and two submarines. He was not provided with carriers to give air cover and close support to his landing troops.

The equipment and armament of the landing force is not known, but it is assumed that they were supported by machine guns and mortars and possibly infantry cannon. Nor is the loading plan known.

Apparently, no American surface opposition was expected; however, the approach of the task force was screened by two submarines at a distance of about 75 miles in advance of the main body. A picket destroyer was posted 10 miles forward of the main body to make the landfall and conduct further reconnaissance. In addition to the absence of fighter air cover, the Japanese seem not to have had a well-developed fire plan for naval gunfire preparation.

Admiral Kajioka's battered task force entered Kwajalein Atoll on December 13th. It was apparent to the Admiral that the difficulty of his mission had been underestimated and that additional means and more favorable conditions must be sought. While repairs were being made to damaged craft he called a conference of his commanders and staff. Reasons for failure were identified as: 1) vigorous seacoast artillery defense; 2) fighter opposition; 3) adverse weather; 4) insufficient Japanese forces and means.

Despite the fact that the same general difficulties were anticipated for the next attempt, the scheme of attack was largely unchanged, a model of inflexibility which seems to have characterized much Japanese planning. The task force was, however, strengthened and reinforced. Two destroyers were assigned to replace the two which had been sunk. One newer, more powerful, destroyer was added. The Maizuru Second Special Landing Force was brought from Saipan and incorporated into the Wake landing force organization. A transport and a float plane tender were also added.

A second task force was formed consisting of two fleet carriers, four older heavy cruisers, two new heavy cruisers and a task force screen of six destroyers. Rear Admiral Abe was placed in command of this task force and was also designated overall commander of forces afloat for the projected operation. Admiral Kajioka remained in command of the amphibious force.

The necessity of prelanding softening was recognized. Commencing on December 21, two days before the landing target date, the aircraft of the carrier division were directed to work over Wake defenses. Order of priority of targets was given as U.S. aircraft, artillery batteries, machine gun positions.

To minimize the effect of our seacoast artillery it was decided to make initial landings by darkness. To be sure that the troops actually landed, regardless of how the battle fared for the forces afloat, the two destroyer-transports were to be run aground on the south shore in the vicinity of the airstrip. Landing barges, each bearing 50 men, would land along the south shore, two on Wilkes, two between the end of the airstrip and Camp One, and two just west of Peacock Point. In the event that this force, approximately 1000 men, was unable to force a landing, a 500-man reserve would be committed. As a last ditch expedient, if all else failed, the destroyers would be beached and their crews would swarm ashore. The Japs were taking no chance of a second failure.

Chapter Six

"All Japs Are Liars"

OUR VICTORY OVER THE Japanese task force simply did not make sense. It was hard for any of us who knew the odds or knew even the rudiments of military theory to realize that it really happened. We knew that the enemy had ships enough that day and men enough to have tied us up in a gift-wrapped package for delivery to Tokyo. Yet the Japanese had thrown away their chance by plain stupidity.

They had plenty of aircraft in the Marshalls, but they brought no air cover for the landing. They made no attempt to subject the island to a real preliminary bombardment. When we did not answer their opening fire, they threw away their decisive advantage of armament by coming close enough for our batteries to engage on comparatively even terms. They made no attempt to threaten more than one sector of the shore, not even by a feint, which might have been expected to force us to divide our strength. They made no attempt to send troops ashore in landing craft. The transports came steaming in with the warships as though they expected their troops to stroll ashore. The whole task force walked right into our trap as though we were going to welcome them with a brass band. It was worse than stupidity. It was suicidal. I am not detracting from the performance of our gunners or pilots when I say that. For when the Japanese had blundered into our trap, our guns and planes hit them so hard, smashed them so fast and so badly that the enemy did not have force enough left to try again with a properly delivered attack.

While we were talking about it, trying to figure out why the enemy had been so stupid, I remembered a bit of wisdom passed on to me by a sage with sergeant's chevrons when I was a young lieutenant, brand-new in China, "All Japs are liars, sir. They can't help lying no more than a dog can help barking."

That was when I first heard the wise fable of the Japanese who was hurrying toward the railroad station with a suitcase when he met his best friend.

"Good morning," said the friend. "Are you going to Nagasaki?"

"Oh, no, indeed. I'm going to Tokyo."

"Ah-ha!" cried the friend in triumph. "Now I *know* you're going to Nagasaki."

That Peking fable, more truth than wit, is to this day the only explanation I have been able to think of that might explain the enemy's stupidity in that attack on Wake. Their planes had bombed and strafed us for three days. From what I have heard of Japanese combat reports, and from what I know of the Japanese propensity for falsehood, I am convinced the Jap pilots must have reported that they had knocked out every position they even flew over. After all, that was what their superior officers wanted to hear, wasn't it? So when the Jap ships opened fire, and when we baited our trap by holding our own fire, the task force commander must have decided that the pilots had been right. So he stuck his head right into the noose.

It was inevitable that the success of our trickery should make the China Marines on Wake retell the classic of the trap at Tsing-tao, a reference to which used to drive the Japanese into chattering rage. In World War I, the Japs sent a Navy task force to attack the German treaty port of Tsing-tao in China. The Japs knew their guns outranged the German shore batteries, so they set a line of buoys to mark the extreme range of the German guns and then stayed safely outside that line while they poured shells into the German positions until the ships broke off the action at nightfall.

That night, the Germans secretly sent out small boats and moved the buoys much nearer the shore. The next morning, moving into position to resume the bombardment, the Japs didn't notice that the buoys had been moved much closer to shore. They were serenely confident they were entirely safe as long as they didn't pass the line, and so they steamed right up to the buoys—and then the Germans shot them up like a bunch of clay pigeons.

There was considerable argument among the old-timers whether the Japs had been dumber at Tsing-tao or when they walked into our trap, but no amount of talk could explain their cowardice in the attack on Wake. When we finally engaged them and they knew the score, the odds were still heavily in their favor, but they didn't even try to make a fight of it. They still should have taken us, but as soon as we opened fire, they turned tail. Some of the destroyers attempted to cover the escape of the larger vessels with smoke screens, but mostly it was every man for himself. Only the panic of cowardice can explain why those fighting ships of the Japanese task force ran off and left the slower transports to get away as best they could. I am not fool enough to indict the whole Jap Navy for the performance of a few, and I do not doubt that many Japanese units showed great courage in combat, but this much I know: the Japanese could have taken Wake Island December 11, twelve days before they did take it. They failed because of their stupidity and cowardice. With, I might add, an assist from a few Marines and the submarine *Triton*.

We were all pretty well set up over our success, but there was no victory celebration on Wake. We had too much to do. We knew the enemy would be back. We knew that if he got ashore in force, we were finished. Nobody said it out loud, of course, but we all knew that sooner or later the Japs would be able to force their way ashore and wipe us out unless we were reinforced. Most of us at that time still believed we would be reinforced, but even the most optimistic private must have remembered that axiom of the Corps which, when I was a private, I once heard put thus:

"Maybe you oughta get more, maybe you will get more, but you all can depend on getting what you already got."

So you make-do with that.

And making-do was another all-night job.

Gunner Hamas trucked out shells, powder and detonators to replenish the supplies of the 5-inch batteries. Work details filled sandbags, strengthened positions, replaced communication lines torn out by shellfire or bombs. On Peale Island, the range-finder and the damaged gun were repaired. On Wake proper, Lieutenant Lewis checked data worked out to enable his 3-inch AA guns to lay beach barrages if the enemy tried a landing. On Wilkes, Captain Platt assigned sectors to McAlister's battery and Gunner McKinstry's volunteers to prepare for infantry defense.

At five o'clock in the afternoon, signals at sea were reported from Peale Island. A smoke bomb released three red balls about thirty feet in the air. They were four thousand yards northeast of Toki Point. At intervals of ten minutes, the signal was repeated twice at the same spot. Then nothing more. Perhaps one of the Jap pilots we had shot down was calling for help, but that is only a guess. We never did find out what the red balls meant.

We buried our dead that night. As men were killed, the bodies had been put in the reefer at Camp Two. Bomb shelters for the living had to take precedence over graves for the dead. Now, we buried them in a common grave in the darkness to hide our casualties from any Jap patrol plane that might fly over.

We had no chaplain. The services were read by a civilian, a Mormon lay preacher. I don't remember his name, but I remember he had a long beard and went around from one place to another during attacks passing out his religious pamphlets. A serene man who gave his pamphlets but never pressed his cause.

Commander Cunningham, Mr. Teters and I were there with the burial party. So was the father of one of the civilian dead. Four Marines from the nearest machine gun emplacement formed a firing squad. The grave was camouflaged before morning.

One grave was apart from the others. It was in the middle of Barninger's battery position. It held the body of the first man of the First Marine Defense Battalion killed in action. In the air attack of December 9, a bomb had landed on the lip of his foxhole, killing him instantly. All they could do was make his foxhole his grave.

They made a small mound and put some chunks of coral on it. They didn't have a book with the burial service in it, but they gathered around the grave. The lieutenant said they would say the Lord's Prayer for his soul. They repeated the prayer after the lieutenant. Some said the Catholic version, some said the Protestant version, and some only moved their lips when they came to parts they weren't sure about. Then they went back to work. That was how they buried Private John Katchak, of Coaldale, Pennsylvania, who was nineteen years old. Lieutenant Barninger, an unsentimental young man, noted in the battery journal: "His grave in the middle of the battery position, serves as a continuous reminder of the task before us and a source of inspiration to us all."

While the dead were being buried, I ordered Godbold's 3-inch battery shifted to the eastern end of Peale Island because I suspected the enemy had spotted their position from the air and because I believed the new position would enable Godbold to oppose any landing attempt that side of the atoll more speedily and with less chance of being cut off. Dan Teters mobilized a couple of hundred civilians to help, but even so the move took all night. For one thing, almost all the sandbags at the old position were so damaged that they had to be abandoned, and we were running out of sandbags to replace them. So Godbold's new emplacements had to be built of bags of cement and ammunition boxes filled with sand.

At 4:45 a.m., December 12, Captain Godbold reported his new position "manned and ready."

About the same time, Captain Tharin took off to make the dawn patrol around the island.

A few minutes later, a Jap patrol plane attacked the island. Low visibility handicapped our AA gunners as the Jap dumped his bombs and strafed, but Captain Tharin pounced on him from above. The Jap tried desperately to get away, but Tharin hung on his tail, machine guns blasting, until the Jap flipped into a dive and crashed into the sea.

A little before noon, the Jap bombers came as usual. Forty of them this time. No matter how many we shot down, they always came back in force. It was rather discouraging, but a man can get used to anything. I think our life at this time, our attitude, was accurately summed up by Lieutenant Barninger's notation for this day, December 12: "Uneventful. Continued to work on foxholes, freshen camouflage, clean the guns and get some sleep. The bombers came, but they are becoming an old story."

There was one important event he did not note. From the first day, when our lack of radar enabled the Japs to hit us such a smashing blow, we had been trying to devise some sort of aircraft detection device. This was a desperate need, for the surf made so much noise on the reefs surrounding the island that normally planes could not be heard until they were almost directly overhead. Consequently, if the Japs again came out of a rain squall as they had the first day, or if they came out of the blinding sun, they could be on top of us before we discovered them.

After a great deal of thought and consultation, we decided a listening horn was the only detection device we had a chance of building with what we had available on Wake. We knew there was a definite formula of curves to keep out extraneous noises, which was why the old regulation listening horns were built with a curved lip, but there was no way on Wake to make an instrument with the proper curves. The best we could contrive was a crude pyramidal box with four uncurved plywood sides.

We tried out our makeshift horn December 12. It didn't work. It brought in too many extraneous noises such as the surf, making these noises an even worse handicap than if we depended on our unaided ears.

To balance this disappointment, however, that was the day Captain Freuler succeeded in a job of improvisation only less important than his trick which enabled the Grummans to carry our only available bombs. In the first day's attack, a major loss even in the air squadron's catalogue of crippling losses had been the destruction of the squadron's entire supply of bottled oxygen. Now Captain Freuler rigged up a makeshift apparatus by which he was able to fill the planes' oxygen containers from the contractor's supply of welding oxygen. I never did understand the process, but it was extremely dangerous. I remember Major Potter reported to me that Captain Freuler risked his life every time he operated the transfer apparatus. I remember, too, that Captain Freuler refused to let anyone else do that job.

The next day, December 13, was memorable on Wake. It was the first day of the war we did not have a raid. The men freshened camouflage, worked on positions, cleaned weapons and caught a little sleep. Some of them even got a chance to take a bath in the lagoon, though that was an after-dark luxury.

In the late afternoon, as Captain Freuler started to take off for the evening patrol, something went wrong with his plane. She swerved suddenly to the left, rushing toward a gang of civilians working with a crane. Freuler fought to swing the ship back on her course, but she wouldn't respond. He tried to force her up, but she had no lift. He fought for control of the ship to the last instant, and then to save civilians working in his path he whipped his plane farther to the left and smashed into the brush. He escaped unhurt, but the plane was a wreck. Even Lieutenant Kinney and Sergeant Hamilton couldn't patch it up again. All they could do was move the wrecked plane over with Elrod's wreck to serve as dummies to entice the Jap bombs. Incidentally, the Japs kept wasting bombs on both dummies.

At dawn one day (I forgot what day it was), as Marines stood to their guns for the morning alert, four Jap flying boats came out of the dimness to attack. Down near Peacock Point, ready at his .50 caliber machine gun, Pfc Michael Olenowski didn't see them. Suddenly he heard a yell:

"Mike! Mike! There they are!"

Pfc Harvey Mosley, standing beside the gun, was pointing upward. Olenowski saw the Japs and whirled with the gun to fire. The swinging gun caught Mosley on the head, knocking him flat as Olenowski cut loose.

That blow on the side of his head did something to Mosley's ear. He kept complaining about it the rest of the battle, but he wouldn't report sick. Men were needed too badly. Not that he got any sympathy from his mates. As Pfc Olenowski said:

"Hell, Mose, you oughta have better sense than to be in the way when you yell a thing like that."

The flying boats were beaten off without damage, but later in the morning the big bombers resumed their daily schedule. This time, they really worked us over. There were forty of them and they were all after the same target. They must have spotted my CP and the other shore dugouts on the previous trip. For beginning at Kuku Point, they walked their bombs straight down the beach toward Camp One.

In the CP, we listened to the explosions coming nearer, nearer. The dugout was eight feet deep, with a roof of heavy timbers mounded over the coral and sandbags, but it seemed paper-thin as we listened to the bombs coming toward us.

A blast shook us. Sand sifted thickly onto our heads from the roof. The next one would be close. All we could do was wait, listening to the belly-freezing whistle a bomb makes coming at you.

Somebody was mumbling.

Then a tight, shrill voice, "What the hell are you doing, Brown?"

And Corporal Brown, "I'm praying, you God-damn fool!"

The next instant the bomb exploded right beside our dugout, but we didn't know that then. We didn't have time to know. There was a blast of flame across the entrance, the stunning force of the concussion, and then the dulled realization that the place was filled with choking clouds of sand falling from the shaken roof. It took a man a moment to realize that he was still alive.

The bombs were falling beyond us now, but the next wave of bombers was coming in, and their bombs were walking toward us down the beach. The ground shook. The explosions stepped over us. And then the bombs of another wave were walking toward us, and all we could do was keep waiting for the next bomb to fall.

Then it was quiet. Men looked at each other as though they could not quite comprehend, and then it was like a great weight lifting from your chest. You wouldn't die today. Not this morning, anyhow.

When we came out of the dugout, I was almost afraid of what we would find. The enemy had plastered that entire stretch of shore so thickly with bombs that one would have thought nothing could have lived through the attack. But we had not lost a man. Except for that single hit on the corner of the CP dugout, every bomb had fallen in the empty spaces between the shelters. It seemed that the only places along that shore where bombs had not exploded were the places where they would have killed Marines. Even if the Japs had been trying to miss us, it didn't seem possible. As one of the men remarked:

"We're sure gonna run out of luck quick if we keep using it up at this rate."

Chapter Seven

When Time Stood Still

IT WAS HARD ON Wake to remember anything except that you needed sleep. The days blurred together in a dreary sameness of bombing and endless work and always that aching need for sleep. I have seen men standing with their eyes open, staring at nothing, and they did not hear me when I spoke to them. They were on their feet. They became so punch drunk from weariness that frequently a man would forget an order almost as soon as he turned away. He would have to come back later and ask what you wanted him to do, and sometimes it was hard for you to remember.

One day as I was leaving for Commander Cunningham's CP, I gave Major Potter some routine instructions. Such-and-such a battery needed twenty men to fill sandbags and another battery needed ten men for some other job—merely a couple of routine matters that he could have handled, without notes or bother, a dozen times a day under normal circumstances. But on this occasion I had no sooner reached Commander Cunningham's CP than Major Potter telephoned to ask what I wanted done about the very things I had told him about hardly ten minutes before.

I repeated the instructions and then turned to Commander Cunningham. I told him, "That's an example of the condition my people are in."

"I know, Jimmy. We'll just have to keep doing the best we can."

That was all anybody could say. There was no use mentioning that unless we got help, our best would not be good enough. That was something you didn't think about. Just as you thought less and less about home, family, your life before the island. A man gets so tired that he stops thinking. Nothing seems to matter as much as sleep.

Perhaps that is why even now it is so hard to remember much that happened during that middle period of the fight for Wake, or even the order of events which we do remember. Each officer made a full report, as best he could remember, when we were finally released from prison camp and in most of them, as in my own, that middle period is a blur in which almost the only certain memory is how much you wanted a whole night's sleep. It is a queer trick of the mind that we can remember clearly the first part of the battle and we can remember the end, but in between was this foggy blur of days and nights when time stood still.

For example, in the reports made later the memories of the survivors have almost unanimously transposed the events of 17th and 18th of December. Wake sustained a major Japanese air attack shortly after noon on December 17th. There is not one single defender who recalled this attack in his post-war account. There is absolutely no doubt that the attack did take place because we reported it to Pearl Harbor by radio shortly after it occurred.

There was the day the bombers centered their attack on Wilkes, and Gunner McKinstry jumped into a flooded foxhole and was almost drowned.

Another day: Lieutenant Kinney had his goggles shot away in a fight in the air, but when he landed he was more concerned about the chances of patching up his precious plane then his narrow escape.

And another: On noon patrol, Lieutenant Kliewer

sighted a formation of enemy bombers approaching the island from the south. Most of our AA fire control equipment had been bombed out by this time, but Kliewer radioed back such accurate altitude that our gunners were able to hit the Japs on the button. The Japs wasted their bombs in their hurry to escape the deadly fire. Two of the bombers were crippled, smoking badly, and three were trailing gasoline as they left. We could be sure they didn't all make it. Then we learned how Lieutenant Kliewer had provided the fire control data that enabled our gunners to smash the attack. He simply flew alone into the midst of the enemy squadron and calmly radioed to the ground the reading of his own instruments while they were shooting at him.

But next day, the bombers were back. No matter how many we shot down, they always came back next day in force—eighteen, twenty, forty and sometimes more. Here is a typical day, as told in a battery report. It happens to be Lieutenant Barninger's for December 15:

"Bombers again combed the island and Peacock Point was heavily hit. No casualties, though the Point was pretty badly torn up. Battery communications were left in such a condition that all wires had to be relaid. Repair was impossible. Bomb hits in the center of battery position shook many of the men in their foxholes, but none was injured. At the airfield, two men were killed by bombs. After effecting repairs, I laid out places for better and deeper shelters.

"During the night, civilians with bulldozers labored with Marines in the construction of two deep shelters with abundance of overhead cover and a topping of three feet of hard coral rock to act as a detonator in case of a direct hit...By morning, the dugouts were completed and the activity of the night erased and camouflage replaced."

Pfc Olenowski was on a .50 caliber machine gun in the path of that attack. They came at him strafing, but he kept firing. He thought he was a dead pigeon, but he was too busy firing to do anything about it. Bullets smacked all around him, but he kept firing. The enemy was out of his field of fire, but he couldn't stop firing. His corporal yelled at him to knock it off, but he couldn't. His left hand was frozen on the trigger. He had to reach over with his right hand and pull his left hand free before he could stop firing. Pfc Olenowski didn't understand it. He had not known a man could be so tired.

Another day, December 16: This is Captain Godbold's report: "The day began at 5 a.m. with guns manned for the dawn alert and men replacing natural camouflage materials." Then these entries:

> *0700*—Continued work on large personnel shelter during the day. Heightfinder shelter completed.
>
> *1330*—One of our fighters reported enemy bombers approaching island from the east at altitude of 18,000 feet. Eighteen bombers in two formations of nine planes each attacked the island. Battery fired 95 rounds. Four planes were smoking heavily as they left the island. One enemy plane was observed crashing into the ocean some distance from the island. Bombs fell in lagoon near the battery.
>
> *1800*—Island attacked by one patrol plane. Bombs fell across road from battery position. Battery position heavily machine-gunned. Due to low visibility, battery did not fire.
>
> *1900*—Set night watch. 75-man working party completed large personnel shelter. Pfc L.N. Schneider and Pvt. A. LePore reported for duty from the Marine garage.

I heard a man talking in the dark. Where the hell were all those reinforcements? When was a guy going to get some sleep? Did anybody ever hear of such a fouled up detail as this was?

A weary voice broke in, "What you beatin' your gums

for? Nobody asked you to join this lash-up. You're a brave volunteer, remember?''

Somebody laughed. Somebody started talking about a liberty he made in Dago and about a blonde whose husband worked at night. I walked quietly on in the dark. An officer need not worry about the morale of men who grouse about their lot and talk about blondes.

Before morning, though, I had plenty to worry about. I had dozed, and about 2:00 a.m. I was awakened by a report that ships were off the island. I stumbled out into a chilly drizzle and climbed on top of the dugout. I could see nothing, but the lookouts on Kuku Point were positive ships were lying off the island. Other posts reported. They were there, all right. The lookouts said there were at least twelve ships. They were close in.

A corporal behind me said, "Maybe they're ours."

I knew they weren't. We had the word from Pearl Harbor: "All surface craft shall be considered enemy craft." I ordered all batteries prepared for action. This was the pay-off. They wouldn't walk into a trap twice.

But the ships steamed off into the darkness. We waited for them to return for the attack, but they didn't. After an hour of waiting, I passed the word that half of the men could sleep beside their guns while the other half maintained security watch. As dawn came, grey through the mist, the sea was empty. Where that mysterious Japanese task force was going or why they did not attack us, we never found out. Lieutenant Barninger found only one other incident that day worth mentioning in his report: "Bombers came over again, but they are becoming commonplace."

The days dragged on, each a smudgy carbon of the day before, except that each day you wanted sleep more badly. I think my own longest stretch of unbroken sleep was two hours during the fifteen days of battle. There were two days that the bombers did not come, and perhaps I got a longer sleep then. I don't remember. I know I kept going on black coffee. I suspect most of the others did, too. I made every effort—not always successfully—to see that all hands got hot coffee, whatever else they missed. My years in the Marine Corps, as an enlisted man and as an officer, had taught me that if a Marine has plenty of hot coffee, he can get along without almost anything else. For a while, anyhow. The trouble on Wake was, it seemed we would have to get along on black coffee indefinitely.

I remember the rats got worse. They overran us. A Marine dozing in his foxhole was as like as not to be awakened by a family of rats moving in with him or just visiting in search of food. During one heavy bombing, a large rat was apparently driven berserk by shell shock. It raced wildly around and around in circles and then dived into a foxhole, attacking the Marine crouched there. The crazed rat bit the man badly, fastening its teeth in his nose, hanging on while he beat it to death. The Marine did not think the incident as funny as his mates did. It is rather difficult to be greatly amused when you have to kill a rat hanging on your nose while trying at the same time to stay low enough in your foxhole to escape bomb fragments.

And the birds—a lot of us never could make up our minds which was the greater pest, the rats or the birds. I remember one day when the ground was littered with hundreds of birds killed by the concussion of a heavy bombing. Instead of being able to rest then, perhaps even get a little sleep, Marines had to gather up the multitude of dead birds and dispose of them as a sanitary precaution.

There were times when an air raid alarm would bring men tumbling out to their guns. Then they would find that some lookout, groggy for sleep, had made a mistake. What he had thought were Jap planes were birds in formation, their wings motionless, soaring high above the island. I doubt that even Mr. Audubon would have remained a bird lover on Wake.

It was during this time that diarrhea hit us. The men

made bawdy jokes about it, but it wasn't funny. Diarrhea can destroy the combat efficiency of troops as surely as enemy fire. As a matter of course when the war began, one of my first orders had been for all units to dig heads—the Navy term for latrines—and to exercise great care in burying all garbage. From time to time, I passed along a reminder, and my observation indicated that most of the military personnel sensibly obeyed the orders for sanitary precautions. We were also able to exercise sanitary control over the civilian volunteers working at Marine positions, but there was nothing we could do to prevent the civilians in the bush from leaving garbage and waste uncovered. We had neither the men nor time to police them. As a result, flies became a danger as well as a pest. We had to fight disease as well as the Japs. We kept the disease in closer check than I had dared hope, but numbers of the men were so weakened by diarrhea that they collapsed and had to be carried to the hospital. I do not know of a single Marine who turned in sick as long as he could drag himself about his job.

We had scattered food caches over the island as a precaution against destruction of our food supply by bombing, but we were still trying to serve two meals daily from a central mess. The mess hall at Camp Two had been destroyed, but Dan Teters' civilian cooks were still able to prepare meals in what was left of the galley. The food was distributed to battery positions by truck, once early in the morning and once in the evening. I ordered that all food distribution should be made under cover of darkness. Otherwise, if a Jap plane happened to pass over, the pilot might spot a camouflaged battery by watching the food trucks.

We had sufficient food for all hands throughout the battle, but there were times when the distribution system fouled up. It was to be expected that this would happen under combat conditions, but that did not make it any more pleasant for the Marines who failed to get their chow. There was, for instance, the case of Corporal

Franklin D. Gross and his machine gun crew away out near Peacock Point. They were supposed to send men to pick up their rations at a distribution point to which the trucks brought the food. But every meal, by the time Corporal Gross's representatives got to the distribution point, there was little or nothing left. The day they brought back only five sandwiches for eight men, Corporal Gross decided that emergency action was required.

The crew was, however, sadly limited in their choice of method. They could not go foraging because they could not depend on the Japs to refrain from attacking until they returned to the guns. So the mission had to be entrusted to a civilian, Sonny Kaiser, who had attached himself to the crew as a handyman.

Mr. Kaiser strolled off and a little later came strolling back with cans of beans, cans of fish, shredded cocoanut, candy and cigars. The Marines, no novices at foraging, looked at him with admiration, but Mr. Kaiser was apologetic.

"This was all I could get," he said.

From that time on, Corporal Gross and his gunners lived very well, indeed. The redoubtable Mr. Kaiser took a little walk every morning and always came back with a good meal and cigar to top it off. The Marines tried to find out how he did it, but he would never tell.

A more individualistic forager was Private Roger Bamford, of Kearney, Nebraska, the youngest Marine on Wake. He looked like a choirboy, with an angelic baby face, and he was, inevitably, called "Chick" by all hands. He had no right to be a Marine at all. The regulations provide that, even with his parents' consent, a youth must be seventeen for enlistment in the Marine Corps. Chick Bamford enlisted on his sixteenth birthday, less than nine months before he was fighting on Wake Island. I did not learn this until after the battle, and by that time it seemed to me that perhaps Private Bamford had earned his place.

Private Bamford did not mind fighting and he did not

mind too much being bombed now and then, but he wanted three meals a day. This two-meals-a-day schedule of Major Devereux's was a lot of nonsense to Private Bamford. He even spent time he could have slept, scouting for extra chow. He finally found a treasure—a large can of chili. The men had been warned against eating too much canned food, but this day, at least, Private Bamford was determined to have a real third meal. After dark, he slipped off alone with his can of chili. That can was supposed to be a meal for thirteen men. Private Bamford ate it all himself. He was a sick boy.

Then there was the Marine who was on a work detail distributing supplies to the scattered caches when he found his load included a case of whisky. He prudently lost it. He lost it very carefully under a pile of brush which he was sure he would be able to locate again.

As I heard long later, without learning the resourceful Marine's identity, he was too busy after that to get back to his private cache, but the thought of his illegal treasure must have been a great comfort to him as he labored and waited for his chance. Each time the Japs came over, the Marine was understandably worried that they might drop a bomb on the "lost" case of whisky, but each time he was relieved to see that no bombs fell in that vicinity. He felt so good about it that he confided his secret to a few close friends and invited them to share his good fortune.

At long last, he had a chance to return to his private cache. He found the brush pile, but the whiskey was gone. I am reliably informed it was days before he quit complaining bitterly:

"This lousy island's full of thieves."

All this time, we were getting Stateside broadcasts about our battle. Though our only remaining means of communicating with the outside world was the radio truck equipment, there were a number of privately owned radio receiving sets on the island, and Marines and civilians gathered around them when they had the chance to hear what the States had to say about us. There was one commentator they always tuned in on, apparently because he got their goat. He had a rich, dramatic voice, and it never seemed as dramatic as when he talked about the Marines on Wake. I did not have an opportunity to listen, but I gathered that we were invariably a "gallant little band," when we weren't "an heroic little band." He seemed to regard us as a squad of Davids clouting a whole army of Goliaths, with one hand tied behind us. His broadcasts caused the Marines to use bad language. Their comments were especially colorful the day he referred to Wake as "the Alamo of the Pacific." Pfc Joe Blow knew enough history to know what happened at the Alamo, and he didn't like the idea.

There was one exception, a young Pfc from Texas. He never missed an opportunity after that to remind his mates, "This is another Alamo, that's what it is." He said it with deep Texan pride, with a satisfaction which Marines from Pennsylvania and Nebraska found themselves unable to share. So they christened him "Sam Houston." After that, I never heard him referred to by any other name. Today, I have forgotten the real name of the little Pfc from Texas. He was "Sam Houston" to everybody despite his patiently repeated explanation that Sam Houston did not fight at the battle of the Alamo.

While on the subject of the broadcasts about Wake, I want to scotch once and for all the misconception which seems to be the most persistent and the most widely believed of all the myths about Wake Island. We heard it first from this fulsome commentator. After an especially adjective-studded report, he quoted me as ending a report of a Japanese repulse with the message, "SEND MORE JAPS."

That was news to me.

One of the Marines said, "Anybody that wants it can sure have my share of the Japs we already got."

He spoke for every man on Wake. We were doing our job as best we could and we would keep on doing it as long as we could, but we were not kidding ourselves. We had all the Japs we could handle and a lot more, too. If we didn't get reinforcements and get them fast, our goose was cooked. It was as simple as that and we all knew it, even if nobody would admit it. In any case, I would not have been damn fool enough to send such an idiotic message.

Since we have come home, I have tried to track down that dispatch and fix responsibility for that particular myth. In prison camp, I heard the scuttlebutt theory that somebody attributed the message to us to justify, in advance, failure or inability to reinforce us. I have never found any evidence that this was true. I have heard also a theory that the words were tacked on to the end of a dispatch as somebody's idea of a joke and that they were mistaken at the receiving end for part of the legitimate message. I have found no proof of this, either. To this day, I don't know who sent that message or why. All I do know is that I did not send it and neither did Commander Cunningham. Beyond that, any man's guess is as good as mine.

Not that we had time to waste thinking about it on Wake. We made a few unprintable comments and went on with our job, fighting off the bombers, preparing for the landing we expected any day. We loaded a barge with a ton of dynamite and anchored it in the small boat channel between Wake and Wilkes. The dynamite was connected to an exploder on the channel bank, and a volunteer was assigned to blow it up if the Japanese started coming ashore. We did not expect that this would seriously check a full-scale attack by the enemy, but it was one more thing that might make his victory costly.

The men still felt sure we would be reinforced, and each day they wondered if this was the day we would get the word when our reinforcements would arrive. Each day, too, we wondered if this was the day of the Jap attack we knew was coming, the all-out assault on the island. We didn't have to wonder about the bombers. They always came. During the entire battle for Wake, there were only two days we were not attacked from the air. But no matter how hard we were hit, no matter how tough the going got, men still came up with a wisecrack.

I remember Pfc Martin, a Southern boy who preferred the nickname "Shorty" to his own, which was Virgil. He was so green a boot when the Japs made their first attack that he stood up to see what was going on. He seemed fascinated by the fireworks as the Japs made a strafing run.

"Say, Sergeant," he asked, "what're those balls of fire?"

"Tracer bullets," said Sergeant Raymon Gragg.

Pfc Martin decided rather quickly that he was a little tired of standing up.

He learned fast, though. The youngsters did on Wake. They learned to take everything the Japs could throw at them—and still manage a wisecrack. Pfc Martin began every day with the same blithe remark. I suppose some people would call it adolescent bravado, nose-thumbing at whatever was coming, but I prefer to call it morale. Every morning as they manned their gun for the alert, Pfc Martin cheerily sang out:

"Good morning, Sergeant Gragg! And I sincerely hope I can say the same thing tomorrow morning."

And I remember, too, a youngster's voice I heard in the darkness before dawn December 17. Thirty years' service is the usual period for retirement in the Marine Corps, but nobody was thinking about retirement that morning. We were awaiting the attack of that Japanese task force that passed us by. The island was tense. Every man must have felt this was the end. There wasn't a sound as we waited. Then, as though he were yawning, I heard the voice of some Marine at a machine gun.

"Oh, well," he said, "it all counts on thirty."

Chapter Eight

The Misfortunes of Sergeant Gragg

EVEN ON WAKE ISLAND we had our laughs. Perhaps it was not very merry laughter, and probably the incidents that seemed funny to us were not really very humorous, but we were grateful for them. They are, of course, only footnotes to battle, but perhaps they will make clearer how it was on Wake. For these were the men who fought the battle.

Sergeant Raymon Gragg had half a dozen years in the Marine Corps and a hitch in the artillery before that. He had once been a wrestler and looked it. I think he came originally from Oregon, but I am told he usually gave his home address on questionnaires as simply: U.S. Marine Corps. He was a fine non-com and he knew his guns as a mother of ten knows babies, but on Wake he was always having embarrassing moments.

Sergeant Gragg was very particular about his feet, a natural trait in a veteran soldier, and he dinned into his men the necessity for caring properly for their feet. Then the sergeant ran out of footpowder. It was hot and grubby fighting on that sun-glazed spit of sand, and a man seldom got a chance to take a real bath, which made footpowder even more of a necessity.

After some miserable days, Sergeant Gragg heard of a supply cache that contained footpowder. The first night he was able to get away for a bath in the lagoon, he visited the cache and groped around in the dark until his hands felt a familiar container. Then he had a bath, sprinkled the powder liberally in his shoes, put them on and strolled back to the battery with an air of satisfied well-being. To top it off, that night they had a chance to get some sleep.

Sergeant Gragg did not remove his shoes, of course, for all hands stretched out fully dressed in case of attack. He dozed off blissfully—and was awaked almost at once. The rats seemed to be holding a convention around him. They crawled over him, and as fast as he knocked them off, they crawled back again. The rare opportunity for sleep was gone before Sergeant Gragg discovered what was wrong. The footpowder he had used in the dark was powdered cheese.

For all I have heard, Sergeant Gragg's skill as an artilleryman was exceeded only by his skill in providing himself with the chocolate bars which were his favorite delicacy. No matter how rugged the going got, no matter how badly we were bombed, Sergeant Gragg always seemed able to find a chocolate bar to munch during a lull. As he munched his bar, he was the personification of perfect morale. No matter what happened, it could not get him down as long as he had a chocolate bar.

At last, Sergeant Gragg had only one bar left. He hoarded it for a special occasion. That came just before the final attack. He sat down and tenderly unwrapped his last chocolate bar. They say that was the only time the morale of Sergeant Raymon Gragg was ever shaken. The bar had worms in it.

Then there was the day the enemy bombers centered their attack on his battery. As gun captain of a 3-inch gun, Sergeant Gragg stood with his earphones on as the bombers came at them. He kept his gun firing until the last possible moment. Bombs were coming down on the position before his crew dived for the shelter. Sergeant Gragg came last, of course. He had to sprint for it. In his haste, he forgot he was still wearing the earphones. The dugout was thirty feet away—and the phone cord was only twenty feet long. The cord stopped the sprinting sergeant so sharply that he was jerked backward off his feet. He didn't have time to try again. He had to lie there in the open, "feeling as naked as a jaybird," while the bombs exploded around him. It was not a soothing experience. Nor were the grins of his Pfc's as they crawled out of the dugout after the raid and inquired solicitously if the sergeant had hurt himself.

Pfc Verne L. Wallace had an even deeper cause for chagrin. He had been assistant manager of a suburban movie house in Philadelphia in 1940 when, over a sociable glass of beer, a friend began boasting that he was going to enlist in the Marine Corps. He jeered at Wallace, a rather slight young man, and offered to bet that the Marine Corps wouldn't take such a scrawny recruit even if Wallace had any idea he might enlist. Just to show he was as good a man physically as his friend, Wallace accompanied him to the recruiting office. The Marines turned down the friend—and took Wallace.

"Every time I'm under fire," Wallace told a pal on Wake, "I keep thinking, 'What the hell am I doing here? I ought to be in Philadelphia!'"

Over on Wilkes Island, Corporal Bernard E. Richardson worried for days about his novel. He had grown up in show business, but what he wanted to be was a writer. When he enlisted he began his novel. It was about the stock companies, tent shows and carnivals which had been his life before he became a Marine. He worked on it every day, no matter how tired he was, slowly piling up the pages of manuscript. His friend, Corporal Brown, told me the novel was almost finished—150,000 words of manuscript—when the war started and Richardson moved out to Wilkes Island with his battery. Days passed before he had a chance to try to rescue his manuscript. Then he learned that a bomb had landed on the tent where he had left it.

Incidentally, after we were in prison camp, Corporal

Richardson began secretly rewriting his novel. I was told that he managed to write about forty thousand words on a weird variety of scraps of paper before the Japs found his manuscript and destroyed it. Corporal Richardson's comment was, "I guess I better stick to short stories till I get home."

Corporal Richardson's ambition was unusual for a Marine, but any man on Wake would have told you that Rip Taylor's ambition was the craziest any man ever had. Pfc Rudolph J. Taylor was sometimes called "Curly" because his head was as bald as a cueball, but usually he was called "Rip" because of his fervent conviction that Rip Van Winkle was the only man he had ever heard of who got enough sleep.

During the battle and the long months in prison, other men's postwar ambitions often changed. A sirloin steak became a more pressing desire than a chicken farm in Iowa or a date with the girl he left behind. Not so with Pfc Taylor. He never wavered in his ambition. The rest of us came to hate the sand and the glare of the sun, but Pfc Taylor's ambition was to have a Pacific island of his own. As he explained it:

"You dopes can beat your brains out if you want to, but me—once they secure this war, I'm going to find me a little island like this and just sit."

I suspect that Sergeant Orville J. Cain was unique on Wake Island. He was a Marine who never used profanity, no matter how great the provocation. I have heard that Sergeant Cain did not curse even when the radio commentator said we had asked for more Japs.

Sergeant Cain had been a prize fighter before he joined the Marines, but that did not explain his religious convictions. He was a good sergeant, an able gun captain, but even before the war his religious beliefs caused him to enforce several rules of his own that were somewhat beyond Marine Corps practice. He would not permit any beer to be drunk in his tent. The men who bunked there with him had to drink their beer elsewhere or do without.

Nor would he permit any poker in the tent nor even matching of dimes. Whatever they may have thought about it, the men in his tent did not argue the matter with him. Sergeant Cain's physique did not encourage objections. The men labeled him "Deacon" and let it go at that.

Deacon Cain never let a day pass without reading his Bible. As he said, the Bible had a lot of good dope in it if a man would only read it. Even after we were fighting, the Deacon still found time to read his Bible, though I have been told he did not need to read it. He could quote it wholesale.

He was the one Marine on Wake nobody ever heard express any animosity toward the Japs. He killed them, but without any unchristian feeling of hatred. Then came the day when the Japs apparently spotted Sergeant Cain's position. They dived in, blasting with everything they had. It was like gunmen shooting it out toe-to-toe.

The first Jap was hit. He was gushing smoke. The others were coming in, spraying the position with fire. The first Jap crashed in flame.

The deacon said, "God bless you, brother!"

And calmly picked another target.

Chapter Nine

The Lucky Dollar

TODAY THE BOMBERS were aiming at Peale Island. Men's nerves pulled taut as they watched the Japs coming at them. It's not easy to remain casual when you know you're the bull's-eye on the target. Only Platoon Sergeant Johnalson E. Wright did not seem to feel the tension. The bombers might have been a flock of sparrows for all the excitement he showed as he went ahead with his job in the director pit, providing data for the firing guns.

The legend was that "Big" Wright was the fattest man in the Marine Corps and that he could drink a keg of beer without assistance. I do not know whether the legend was true or whether he actually did weigh 320 pounds as they said, but I would not have given odds against it. For Platoon Sergeant Wright was the kind of man of whom anything might have been true, an epic figure, a Falstaff without bombast, a professional soldier who did his job of fighting as calmly as he took a nap.

Now the Japs were almost on top of them. They were gliding in for the kill. This time the Japs were laying the bombs right in their lap. A jittery kid was saying something. Cursing, maybe. Or praying. Or maybe just saying something, not even knowing what it was, in the tight, shaky voice of a man at the breaking point.

Big Wright didn't bother to turn his head. He said, "Knock it off, Chick. Wait till you're hurt before you holler."

Not a memorable line, nothing dramatic about it, and his voice was casually matter of fact, but the kid shut up. That can happen, like cold water thrown in a man's face, and it can jerk him back from the edge of panic. It can stiffen a man to keep at his job when the world blows up under his feet. Knowing what to say and how to say it is one of the things that make good sergeants.

There on Peale Island, the last minute came. In another moment, the bombs would be coming down on top of them. In just another moment—

"Okay," Wright said. "Hit the hole."

The men scuttled for the tiny entrance of the bomb shelter, scrambling in their haste to get underground. Platoon Sergeant Wright did not try to follow them. He squatted ponderously, calmly in a corner of the director pit as the first Jap let go his bombs. He took something from his pocket and held it tightly.

"Hey, Godwin!"

He was doing it again, singing out to Platoon Sergeant William Godwin as he did every time they were bombed.

"Don't you worry, Godwin! I'm squeezing my lucky dollar for you!"

Somebody laughed. Somebody always did, even though the bombs were whistling down. Then the bombs began exploding. The concussion jolted Wright in the director pit, and sand and bits of coral rained down upon him, but he just hunched there in the corner of the pit, squeezing his lucky dollar.

Then the Japs were gone, and Big Wright stood up, dusting off the sand. He put his dollar back in his pocket. The men came crawling out of the shelter and somebody said the lucky dollar had worked again.

"It always works," Wright said.

Nobody knew where Big Wright got his lucky dollar nor why it was supposed to be lucky, but men who had done duty with him years before said he had carried it as long as they could remember; that he always said it was what brought him alive through the Nicaragua campaign. It was something to talk about. Men could argue endlessly whether there could be such a thing as a good-luck charm, a magic talisman. Most of them said it was a lot of bunk, but when the bombers came, even the scoffers felt easier being near Big Wright as he squatted in the director pit and squeezed his lucky dollar. He could have crawled into the dugout with the others, of course, but he said he was too fat for that. Anyhow, he didn't need a bombproof as long as he had his dollar. Maybe he was kidding, maybe not; but out of such things morale is built. It stiffens green troops to see an old soldier who knows the score, just calmly sitting out the worst the enemy can throw at you. As for his lucky dollar, there was one argument nobody could answer—they were still alive and how could anybody prove it wasn't the dollar that did it?

Pfc Bernard A. Dodge thought about it a lot and finally got a lucky coin of his own. He couldn't find a silver dollar, so he used a fifty-cent piece. When the Japs came over, when Wright called to Godwin that he was squeezing the dollar for him, Pfc Dodge would crouch in the generator pit and squeeze his own coin for luck. Maybe it was crazy, but it was something to hang onto, and there are times when a man needs that.

So the days dragged on, and every day the bombers came to hammer us; to beat us down, break us for the landing we expected every dawn. By December 19, they were using lots of heavier bombs: 1,000-pounders. They left craters seven feet deep and thirty feet wide.

Men wondered in bitter bewilderment why reinforcements didn't come. Or why they had to hold the island, anyway. Let the Japs have it. What the hell good was it?

Platoon Sergeant Wright squelched them, "You ain't paid to think, Mac. All you're paid to do is fight where they tell you to.''

I suppose that was as near as we came to an orientation lecture on Wake Island, but it seemed to suffice. The Marines did not need a lot of lectures and pamphlets to make them understand our war aims. As far as they were concerned, there was only one thing we were fighting for. It was quite simple: to win. Or as Big Wright would have said, ''This war's just part of the job, like guard duty or close order drill or spit-shining your shoes.'' I think that summed up the attitude of most of us, officers and men.

As the days passed, the enemy hit us harder and harder. And we had less and less power to strike back. We still had ammunition, but I cautioned against waste. We did not have enough to last indefinitely. We did have plenty of food and water.

Since my return to the States, I have found a widespread misconception that shortage of water was the reason more troops were not put on Wake. The truth is that our seawater distillation plant and the catchment system for rain water provided more than enough fresh water for every possible purpose at all times. Our water allowance was around fifteen gallons per man per day, and in the field you can do with one gallon per man per day without any trouble. We had fully two million gallons in storage when the war began, and there was never at any time any danger of a shortage. Whatever the reasons for not having a stronger garrison on Wake may have been, lack of water was not one of them.

Major Putnam's squadron still took to the air to oppose every daylight attack, but now they were down to two planes. No. 10 and No. 12. By working all night and part of the day, Lieutenant Kinney and Sergeant Hamilton somehow got the scrapheap remnants of No. 8 in shape to fly. There was another battered wreck, No. 9, which they might be able to get off the ground except for the minor fact that it did not have an engine. So Kinney and Hamilton began trying to assemble an airplane engine from the burned parts of the planes which had been destroyed the first day.

They were still trying next day when the bombers came over. No. 10 got a direct hit and burst into flames. The Japs were still dropping bombs, but Kinney and Hamilton sprinted to the burning plane and began removing the engine. At any moment, the fire might reach the gas tank, but they needed that engine. They were scorched and blackened by the fire, but they got the engine out—and installed it in No. 9.

And then, by working most of the night again, by switching parts and improvising out of bits of junk, they wrought another miracle. They created a plane out of baling wire and hope, and next day we got the thrill of seeing FOUR planes take off to meet the raiders. And there were only twenty Japs.

All this time, the maintenance of communications— the nerve system of any force in battle—was an increasingly serious problem that had to be solved anew each day and frequently several times a day. Every day some of our communications lines were bombed out and had to be repaired or replaced. Every night some of the lines were chewed up by tractors of working parties. Whenever it happened, day or night, some of our skeleton crew of communications men had to go searching until they found the breaks in the telephone lines. Sometimes they found the trouble quickly; sometimes they had to follow out miles of wire before they found the gaps. Sometimes repairs were a simple splicing job, but oftener the task took hours. Nobody on Wake was more overworked than Technnical Sergeant Randolph June's communications men and their civilian helper, Ham Shoneigh, a volunteer.

A vital part of their job was maintaining our air raid warning network. This was a complete telephone system independent of the regular communication lines. This warning network was set up because we usually could not know of a raid until the planes were in sight. The principal lookouts and all unit positions were on the network. I ordered that the lines should be kept open at all times and that a man should be listening at each phone constantly. In this way, if approaching Jap planes were sighted, the warning could be given immediately and simultaneously to all positions. We had some trouble with the network, there being occasions when one or more phones would not function for both transmission and reception, but the system saved us many casualties.

Like everyone else, the communications men became groggy from exhaustion, but they snapped to it whenever a line was reported dead or when an operator on the warning network reported that he could transmit messages or could not hear anything. The communications men did not wish to wait until a bombing attack was over before hurrying from shelter to repair the lines, but I ordered them not to leave cover until the all clear. It seemed to me that as long as the Japanese attack was only from the air, a few minutes' delay in repairing lines was not sufficiently serious to justify the risk of lives. Even then almost the first thing I heard after the bombs stopped falling was Sergeant June's order to get going.

There was another reason why I warned all hands against leaving cover until the Japs were gone. I suspect many people on Wake thought I was hipped on this subject, and perhaps I was, but it seemed to me an essential, if a rudimentary precaution. I was convinced that the Japs had discovered that we had dugouts along the beach because some men always seemed to forget that they should not leave vehicles parked in plain sight when they drove down to see me or performed some other errand. For the same reason, I did not want the communications men rushing out while the departing Japs were near enough to photograph them.

During this time, when men were becoming punch drunk from exhaustion, my lack of an adequate staff became an especially difficult handicap. Because I had no commissioned officers to do the jobs, Technical Sergeant June was my communications officer and Quartermaster Sergeant Vincent Kleponis was battalion quartermaster. They were excellent men, but still they were only sergeants and every day they were faced with questions that had to be decided by an officer. Ordinarily, with even a skeleton staff, most of those decisions would have been made by the officer in charge of each section. As it was, all such questions had to be brought to me or to Major Potter. It was another reason why even when things were quiet, we could not expect more than a short nap before being awakened to answer some question, settle some problem that would have been taken care of by a lieutenant if I'd had a staff. I am afraid there may have been one or two moments when I reflected with some regret that I might have been a farmer, but I am not sure. I think that usually everybody was too tired to think much about anything except the immediate job that had to be done.

Then came December 20. That was a great day on Wake. There was no raid, and we were grateful for the bad weather that kept the Japs away. I heard a couple of drenched Marines talking as they worked. One was griping, but the other said:

"You can have your goddamn sunshine. This is wonderful weather."

The rains on Wake were almost always brief squalls, however, and the weather soon cleared, but apparently it was still bad where the Japs were. At any rate, they skipped us. That was the second of the two days we were not bombed.

That was a great day on Wake for another reason, a far more important reason to us. That was the day a PBY arrived from Pearl Harbor. We knew it was coming and it was hard to hide the strain of waiting, of wondering what word the PBY would bring. Was it the first of our reinforcements? Were they sending us something to fight the war with? To hold the island with?

Would they send it in time to meet the landing we expected every day? I tried not to think about it because it didn't do any good and there was work to do, but I couldn't keep it out of my head. I don't think any of us who knew the PBY was coming could think of much else except of that plane that was flying toward us. I had passed the word from the first that we were bound to be reinforced. This seemed to me necessary because it is not good if men feel they have been written off as lost. No man fights as well when he feels he has been forgotten. As for what the officer feels, that is his problem; something to be kept to himself. An officer can feel fear and bitterness as deeply as any private, but that also he must keep to himself. The men are looking to him. He must be the man with all the answers even when he doesn't know them or even if there aren't any. It is sometimes rather lonely to be an officer, but Big Wright's crack goes for him just as much as for the complaining Pfc:

"So what, Mac? You're getting paid for it, ain't you?"

Still, it was hard to take, day after day, trying to fight a war with less equipment than we would have had for maneuvers. It was hard to keep on with almost every man doing two men's work. Men can't go on forever without sleep. Time was running out.

I remember the night Captain Elrod stopped at my CP. He had helped smash the raid that day. He had shot it out with a Jap in the sky, and the Jap had gone down, and Elrod had nursed his ramshackle plane safely back to the field. Now he had a question to ask. Just one.

"Why the hell doesn't somebody come out and help us fight?"

I couldn't answer him.

Now we were waiting for the PBY, and maybe it would bring the answer to Hank Elrod's question. It was like waiting for Santa Claus, but some of us were cursing him before he arrived. The radioman reported that the PBY was sending out hourly weather reports in English, and a disgusted Marine officer blew up:

"That damn fool must think he's on a picnic. Why doesn't he just invite the Japs to come get him?"

We expected Jap planes, and you couldn't have got a bet on the PBY's chances of not being intercepted, but the pilot must have been humpbacked with luck. That day the Japs just weren't around, and he landed safely in the lagoon, taxiing to the Clipper dock.

A few dirty, dog-weary Marines watched the pilot climb out. He was a reserve ensign, spick and span, and he had a natty overnight bag with him. The others climbed from the plane. They were all ensigns. To the Marines, their lack of rank made that PBY look pretty expendable. Somebody wisecracked, "We must be on a hotter spot than I thought."

The spruce young pilots strode up to the grubby Marines and demanded:

"Where's the Wake Island Hotel?"

The Marines just looked at him. It took him a little while for that question to seep through the weariness of twelve days of battle and lack of sleep. The ensign was about to get impatient when a Marine answered:

"Sir, that's it."

He pointed to a bomb-shattered shambles, all the Jap bombers had left of the hotel, and I heard that all the rest of the day he kept inquiring why somebody didn't tell the people there was a war on Wake Island.

The PBY brought a message from Admiral Bloch to Commander Cunningham. I understand that the message was sent by plane instead of radio because of the fear that at that time the Japanese had broken our code. That message was like a shot in the arm for us.

We should prepare at once to receive aircraft.

We should prepare to evacuate all of the civilians except 250 key personnel.

We should have the civilians ready to be evacuated December 24.

(Left) Occupation forces raise the
Japanese flag on Wake Island.
(Above) A detachment of soldiers
pay homage to a memorial erected
to Unit Commander Uchida, who
was killed in the landing on
Wake Island. Both photos are
from a Japanese picture book.

(Top) The graveyard for planes of VMF 211 on Wake Island. Having fought until they were beyond salvage and repair, these are the remains of the Grumann Wildcats. *(Bottom)* Covered revetment for Marine Corps' plane is examined by Japanese victors. Both photos from Japanese picture book.

SHANGHAI INTERNMENT BARRACKS

November 2, 1942.

This is to certify that James Orlo KING, whose signature appears below, is a Private First Class in the United States Marine Corps.

James Orlo King

J.P.S. DEVEREUX, Major, U.S. Marine Corps.

Aerial view of Wake Island, *above,* taken during allied bombardment on March 11, 1944. *(Below)* When a POW was shipped to another camp, he was issued an "identification slip," of which James Devereux writes, "It was something to remind him he was an American and a Marine, still part of something and not alone, whatever the Japs did to him. There are men who still treasure those scraps of paper." The I.D. slip pictured was provided by James O. King.

收容所へ急ぐ大鳥島の捕虜

U.S. Marine Corps Photo

Taken prisoner on Wake Island, American civilian construction workers are on their way to prison camp.

One of many "Wake Island" envelopes issued during the war to spur greater productivity on the home front.

Capt. P. T. Bahry, Jr., USMC

WORK FOR VICTORY

WAKE

with the **FIGHTING SPIRIT** of the **WAKE ISLAND MARINES**

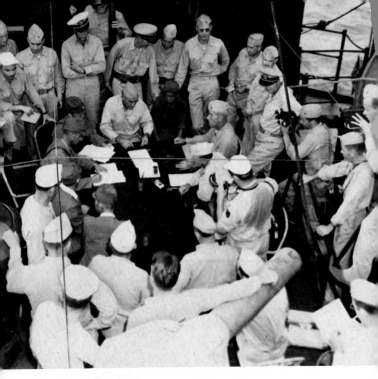

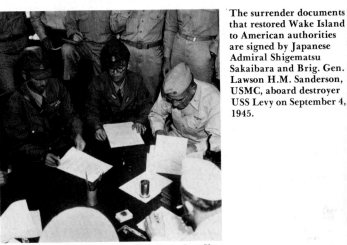

The surrender documents that restored Wake Island to American authorities are signed by Japanese Admiral Shigematsu Sakaibara and Brig. Gen. Lawson H.M. Sanderson, USMC, aboard destroyer USS Levy on September 4, 1945.

U.S. Marine Corps Photos

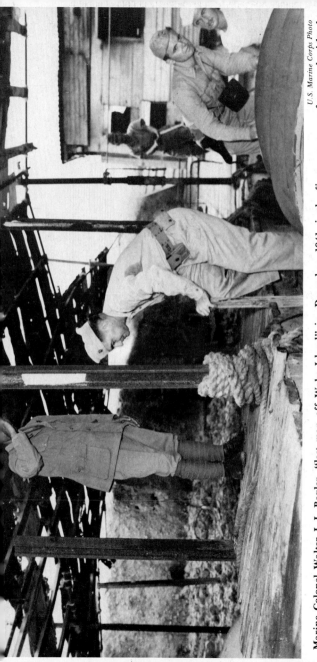

U.S. Marine Corps Photo

Marine Colonel Walter L.J. Bayler, "last man off Wake Island" in December, 1941, is the first man to set foot on the island after the surrender documents were signed.

Before a contingent of U.S. Marine, a U.S. Navy Honor Guard, and assembled Japanese prisoners, the Stars and Stripes are raised over Wake Island on September 4, 1945.

I was not told that the message promised us reinforcements at the same time, but it may have. Certainly we believed so. To us, the instructions added up to only one thing—we were being reinforced. In four days, ships would arrive to take the civilians. We naturally assumed our reinforcements would arrive on those ships. And we must be getting planes since we were ordered to prepare to receive them. The feeling we got, our assumption from the portions of the message passed on to us, was that the high command had decided to make a real fight for Wake.

A task force built around the aircraft carrier *Saratoga* had been operating to the east of Wake, but previously had been restricted from coming nearer than the two hundred miles to the island. Now that task force was being permitted to come to us. I did not know that at the time, but it did not take any mental feat to guess it.

The PBY officers were bunked in the dugout which Mr. Teters shared with Commander Keene. I met them there that night. For the first time, we got a clear picture of the extent of the damage done at Pearl Harbor. It was a jolt. That there had been lack of coordination and cooperation between the Army and Navy was not, however, a surprise to any of us who had done duty in Hawaii.

I think that was when we learned that, according to the Japanese, we were all dead or prisoners. The Japanese radio in Shanghai had claimed the capture of Wake, December 8. They were still claiming it. An officer said, "There's always some dope that doesn't get the word."

It was a laugh, tired as we were. We felt pretty good that night. We no longer felt like men sitting on the end of a limb that somebody was sawing off.

Major Bayler had been sent to Wake on temporary duty to set up the squadron's air-ground communication system and now his mission was completed. His orders were to return via the first available government transportation, and the PBY was it. There was some talk of evacuating Mr. Havenor, the passenger who missed the Clipper, but they didn't have a parachute or life jacket for him, so he missed his second chance to stay out of a Jap prison camp. It was decided that the PBY should take off early next morning in the hope that it would be safely away before the Japs came calling. We knew they would come. They wouldn't give us two holidays in a row.

I walked back to my CP and wrote a hasty report in a letter to Colonel Bone to be carried back by the PBY. It was rather more frank than a formal report might have been because Colonel Bone was my personal friend as well as my Commanding Officer. Naturally I showed the letter to Commander Cunningham and he approved it.

I wrote that he could be proud of the officers and men of his battalion, and that I would take care of them to the best of my ability, but I pointed out that if the high command wanted to keep the island we must have radar and patrol planes as well as other reinforcements.

Then I got something off my chest that had been irking me for days. While we were fighting to hold Wake, we kept getting silly messages from Pearl· Harbor. Somebody back there apparently thought what we needed was an order for all personnel to wear long trousers and keep their sleeves rolled down as a protection against bomb blasts. Then there was the message about window glass. We were taking a beating, dead for sleep, living in holes in the ground, trying to hang on under the daily ceaseless pounding of the bombers—and Pearl Harbor's helpful suggestion was that if we lacked glass to put in our barracks windows, seismograph paper was an excellent substitute.

While the messages may not have been important, I wrote Colonel Bone that they indicated how some people in Pearl Harbor were thinking. It seemed to me, I wrote, that the brass hats who thought up these silly messages had better get down to earth or down in the earth as we were. It may have been making a mountain out of a molehill, but I felt very strongly about such idiotic messages when we were fighting for our lives, and we didn't want to get any more of them.

I felt better with that out of my system. I started a letter to my wife and Paddy, my son. There was much I wanted to tell them, deeply personal things, and some things that seemed important to me I wanted to tell my son in case I didn't come through, but I did not seem able to put any of it down on paper. I wrote a few words and then sat staring at the paper a long time. Then I tore it up. I had work to do.

I kept wondering that night if the reinforcements would reach us in the ships being sent to evacuate the civilians December 24, if they would reach us before the Japanese made another attempt to land. Next morning, two hours after the PBY took off for Midway, I wondered the same thing with deeper concern. For at 9:00 a.m., December 21, we were hit for the first time by carrier-based planes. That meant a Jap task force was closing in on Wake.

Only one Wildcat was in commission and it was on the ground when the Japs struck. There were three flights of dive bombers, escorted by fighters. Gunner McKinstry counted thirty bombers in the raid.

Major Putnam was at Commander Cunningham's CP, but he ran to his car and started back. The dive bombers swooped down on him. He had to stop his car and dive into a ditch beside the road while the Japs scythed around him with strafing fire. Then he raced on to the airfield and took off in our lone plane in an attempt to overtake the departing Japs. The patchwork plane just wasn't good enough, and he had to turn back. It requires real guts to take off when the enemy is right overhead.

Rain and low visibility had prevented effective anti-aircraft fire, but the weather had cleared by the time the

Japs came back for a second raid at 2:30 p.m.

This time, the brunt of the attack was thrown at Peale Island. In the director pit, Big Wright kept his crew on the job until the last minute.

The first bombs were coming down as they ducked for the shelter; as Big Wright squatted in the pit and took out his silver dollar.

"Hey, Godwin!"

There he went again.

"Don't you worry, Godwin! I'm squeezing my lucky dollar for you!"

The bombs landed in the battery position. Crouching men felt the ground heave under them. Some were hit, and the air was clouded with sand and smoke. The blast blew most of the clothes off Sergeant Steve Fortuna. He was sandblasted like a building that is being cleaned, blinded temporarily by the blast of sand, left gasping on the ground. He staggered to his feet, groping in blindness, calling out to Big Wright; calling to find out whether his pal Wright was hit. One of the wounded was moaning, but Big Wright didn't make a sound. He was dead, the lucky dollar still tightly clutched in his hand.

The wounded were carted to the hospital, and then they buried Big Wright. After that was done, Pfc Dodge walked down to the lagoon alone. He stood there a moment turning his lucky fifty-cent piece between his fingers. Then he flung it as far out into the lagoon as he could and walked back to the guns.

Chapter Ten

December 22

MAYBE PFC DODGE WAS RIGHT. Maybe our luck had run out. Major Putnam's limping Wildcat had not been able to fly far enough to search out for the Jap task force, but the attack by carrier-based planes meant that it was close by. The size of the dive bomber squadrons told us plainly as words that it was a powerful force. If reinforcements were going to do us any good, we had to get them right now. Most of us were confident we would be reinforced when the ships arrived to evacuate the civilians, but that was two days away. That might not be soon enough. Meanwhile, I had to make my plans to oppose the enemy's landing on the basis of what I had.

I could not possibly hope to cover all of twenty miles of coastline with the men and weapons at my disposal, so my job was to outmaneuver the Jap commander; to determine the most probable place he would try to come ashore and be ready for him there. I would not have a second chance.

The reefs seemed to answer the question. Except for the tiny break near the small boat channel, the ragged coral reefs surrounded the entire island, but the barrier was much closer to the shore along the southern side of Wake and Wilkes than anywhere else. If the enemy could get across the reefs there, he would be almost on the beach. Once ashore there, he would have a shorter distance to drive to the airfield than from almost any other spot where he might land. So I reasoned that the enemy's main attack would hit us somewhere along the shore between Peacock Point and Kuku Point. If he had the force I thought he had, he probably would try to gain footholds at several points simultaneously. We took what steps we could to strengthen our defenses along the southern shore, though by this time there was not much more we could do than we already had done. Even in the best days on Wake, we had had to scrape the barrel, with the placing of a single gun or a single squad a major problem because they were needed in half a dozen places at once. In retrospect I fully realize I made many mistakes. And these were not our best days.

I expected the enemy to make feints or even diversionary landings at other spots and I thought it probable he would—as, in fact, he did—send patrols in rubber boats into the lagoon to land behind us. I was confident we would be able to keep such moves from becoming a serious threat, but there was always the chance the Japs might make a strong landing attempt at other points as well as on the shore where they were expected. We had to guard against that chance. I had to spread my force out desperately thin to do this, and still there were big gaps we could cover only with a patrolling rifleman or two. I shifted some positions, both to lessen the danger that those men might be cut off by Japs slipping ashore behind them and also to enable me to draw on them more quickly for reinforcements if the enemy broke through our main concentrations along the southern beach. "Main concentrations" seems a little ludicrous under the circumstances. Captain Platt had sixty Marines on Wilkes Island. The shore of Wake proper, from the channel to Peacock Point, was defended by about eighty-five Marines and a handful of volunteers. That was the best I could to do to defend our front door without leaving a back door wide open for the Japs to walk in.

Until the enemy did make his bid for the island, we could expect increasingly heavy attacks from the air. We still had more .50 caliber machine guns that we could properly man, but these alone could not hold off the bombers. Our chances of keeping them from blasting us off the island depended on our ability to keep up effective 3-inch anti-aircraft fire. As I mentioned, from the start of the battle the possible fire power of our 3-inch batteries had been cut in half by lack of adequate fire control equipment and personnel. Volunteer crews had enabled us to improve this a little, but now the 3-inch batteries were even more badly crippled by loss of irreplaceable equipment. The bomb that killed Big Wright also destroyed the battery's director. Now Lieutenant Lewis had our only director and Captain Godbold our only height finder.

I decided to concentrate our 3-inch fire power in Lieutenant Lewis' position and so the night of December 21 I ordered Captain Godbold to send Lewis one gun, the height finder, his power plant, and personnel to man them. The gun from Godbold replaced the gun Lewis had left mounted for beach defense south of the airfield. Thus, for the first time, we had in action in one position a full 3-inch battery of four guns—for Wake—adequately manned.

That was rather like putting most of my eggs in one basket, but it was the only thing to do: the most efficient way to operate our remaining AA battery. The raid in which Big Wright was killed had shown us that the Japs had spotted Godbold's position on Peale Island while Lewis' position on Wake was still undiscovered. In my opinion, Lewis' well-concealed position on the lagoon side of the horseshoe toe was the best position on the island. It was placed so that even if the Japs did discover the battery and attacked, the chances were that a large percentage of the bombs would land harmlessly in the lagoon.

That night of December 21, I also shifted two of God-bold's remaining guns to a new position on Peale, direct-ing him to emplace them for beach defense. His fourth gun was left in the old position, which the Japs had spotted, and dummy guns were set up so the enemy would think the battery was still there. I ordered the crew of this fourth gun and Gunner McKinstry's two re-maining 3-inch guns on Wilkes Island to open fire when-ever any Jap planes appeared. They had to fire by local control, almost blind guesswork, and I did not expect them to hit anything. I gave that order because they were targets the enemy had located and so by lively fire they might deceive the bombers.

It was an order I did not like to give. But it seemed to me justified, even necessary, because it might give Lewis' battery a better chance of escaping discovery and damage. Our anti-aircraft defense depended on keeping Lewis' battery in action.

Peale was now defended by a garrison of less than one hundred Marines plus a group of civilians who had been trained under Marine noncommissioned officers to act as one of Battery D's gun crews. Of them, Captain God-bold later said, "The civilians who served with this strongpoint were of inestimable value. Under the capa-ble leadership of Sgt. Bowsher, they were soon firing their gun in a manner comparable to the Marine-manned guns. Before the surrender of the island, some of these men were slated to be evacuated to Honolulu; however, the entire gun crew offered to stay on the is-land and serve with the battery."

The 5-inch batteries remained as they were. I could not expect the enemy to walk into a trap as they had done the first time, and I knew their ships would be able to stand off, out of range of our guns, and shell us at will, but there was nothing I could do about that. It was possible that instead of shelling the island, instead of making a power drive to win a landing, the enemy might try to sneak ashore in force under cover of darkness. Either way, we were in for a bad time unless reinforcements arrived before the Japs did, and every man on the island knew it.

Yet when I made an inspection, checking the disposition of my forces, I noticed a strange thing. It was an unspoken thing, intangible, but it was as real as the sand or the guns or the graves. My men were average Marines, and they had bitched and griped among themselves like any soldiers. Now their nerves and bodies had been sapped by two almost sleepless weeks. Now the chips were down for the last roll of the dice, and they knew it, and they knew the odds were all against us, but now they were not grumbling. There seemed to grow a sort of stubborn pride that was more than just the word "morale." I have thought about it many times since then, trying to put in words how it was on Wake as our time ran out, and the best I can do is put down two simple things that happened.

Men were working in the darkness, placing sandbags about a gun. Their talk was a weary mumble, but then one voice cut sharply through the dark:

"Aw, nuts! We can take the little bastards the best day they ever lived."

Then there was "Moss" Miller, Corporal Hershal L. Miller, gun captain of a 3-inch crew. Twenty-five rounds a minute is a good rate of fire for a 3-inch gun, but Miller drove his crew to fire faster and faster every time the Japs came over. There toward the end, we got a report at the CP that Corporal Miller had met a Jap attack with fire of thirty rounds a minute. That was faster than I thought possible, even for a fresh crew under perfect conditions, and probably the count was exaggerated, but Marines who saw it said Corporal Miller was firing faster that day than they ever saw a 3-inch fired before.

Then the Japs were gone, and Miller sat wearily down, his shoulders slumping. Somebody said he'd really been pouring it on, and Miller glanced up. His eyes were dead in his head and all he said was:

"If they want this island, they gotta pay for it."

By 1:00 a.m., December 22, the transfer of Godbold's gun and equipment to Lewis' battery was completed and Captain Godbold reported his two guns set up for beach defense.

At the airfield, work went on through the night on revetments for the desperately needed planes we expected, the planes Pearl Harbor instructed us to prepare to receive. Lieutenant Kinney was so weakened by diarrhea he could hardly keep his feet, but he refused to turn in at the hospital. He and Sergeant Hamilton worked most of the night and wrought a final miracle out of their piles of junk, one more plane that would fly. One developed engine trouble, however, so Second Lieutenant Carl Davidson took off alone for the midday patrol. An hour later, Kinney and Hamilton finally coaxed the dead engine into life and the second plane wheezed into the air with Captain Freuler at the controls.

A little before noon, Captain Freuler was scouting south of the island when Davidson called him by radio. Enemy planes were coming in from the north. Again carrier-based dive bombers with fighter escort. Eighteen dive bombers this time. Davidson was attacking.

Freuler swung north of the island to join the battle. He thought he saw a Jap going down under Davidson's fire, but he was too busy to make sure. He had six of the Jap fighters on his own hands at twelve thousand feet.

On his first pass, he got a Jap. The Jap dropped out of formation, smoking thickly as the pilot lost control, as it dropped faster toward the sea. The other Japs broke formation, maneuvering for position. Freuler swung back for another pass. He caught another in his sights. The others were closing in on him from above and behind, but he could only take them one at a time. The second was wobbling, going down, and Freuler pulled out of his pass just in time to escape collision. The falling jap exploded fifty feet below him. The blast of flame was so close that Freuler's plane was badly scorched. The force of the explosion flung his plane crazily upward. He had to fight to regain control. The manifold pressure was dropping. The ship responded sluggishly to the controls. A Jap was on his tail, riddling his plane, and the Wildcat was too badly crippled to dodge.

His plane was a seive. Nobody could figure out later how Freuler lived through the riddling fire. Bullets hit him in the shoulder and the back.

Another Jap was closing on him from behind. He couldn't maneuver. He couldn't escape. He was a fish in a rain barrel.

He took the only chance he had. It looked like suicide in a plane so sluggish, so badly crippled, but he plunged into a steep dive, and the Jap didn't follow. The Jap must have chalked him up as certain, but somehow Freuler managed to pull out of the dive. Somehow he got his plane headed for the field.

Freuler had caught one last glimpse of Davidson. The lieutenant was diving on a Jap with another Jap on his own tail. Freuler was helpless, his plane dying in the air, useless for combat, and all he could do was try to nurse her home. The plane made the field with its last gasp. When the wounded pilot pulled himself out of the plane on the strip, it was a hopeless wreck.

Meanwhile, the dive bombers had worked us over. They took the bait of the 3-inch guns firing by local control and spent much of their bomb load trying to blast those guns.

We waited all afternoon for Lieutenant Davidson to return to the field, but he never came back. He had gone down fighting alone out there at sea. Our last plane was gone. Major Putnam came to my CP to tell me.

"So we're reporting as infantry," he said.

Lieutenant Kinney wanted to volunteer, too, but they

carted him to the hospital. The diagnosis was, "severe diarrhea and complete physical exhaustion."

So another night came and Wake was still ours. Maybe we were going to make it. Just one more day to get through. Then we would know. Then the ships would arrive to evacuate the civilians. Maybe they would bring reinforcements, but we could not be sure. Perhaps we were assuming too much. And that Jap task force would not wait forever before they tried to take us.

Thinking about it didn't help. It was better to try to get a little sleep.

Chapter Eleven

December 23

IT WAS STILL EARLY THE NIGHT of December 22 when lookouts began reporting "a hell of a lot of lights" northwest of the island.

I went outside and climbed on top of the dugout to observe them. The lights were coming in vivid flashes from far beyond the horizon. We had seen occasional lights blinking at sea for a couple of nights, apparently signals between scouting elements of the Jap task force we knew was near the island, but now the flashes of light were so bright, so numerous, and continued so long that we began to think a naval battle was in progress.

Men argued the chances as we watched. The American task force coming to evacuate the civilians was not due until sometime December 24, but maybe it had come on ahead of schedule. Maybe the ships we expected to bring us reinforcements had run into the Japanese force that had been bombing us for two days, softening us for a landing. Maybe our necks were being saved by a sea battle fought too far away for us to hear the guns.

Corporal Brown said, "I'll settle for that for Christmas."

Somebody said, "You and me both."

But if the flashes were not gunfire, if the lights were

illumination by the Japanese, it meant the enemy was there in great force and that he was up to something. It meant, perhaps, that tonight he was coming.

Whatever was happening out there miles away from Wake, it was fixing the odds on our chances of staying alive, only we couldn't read them. The men watching in the dark could wonder what the flashes meant or they could guess, but none of us could be sure of more than the Marine who said, "If that ain't a battle, it's sure a potful of Japs."

We watched the flashes lessen and finally cease, and again there was only darkness on the sea. If the enemy wanted to sneak in on us, he had a good night for it. The weather was kicking up. The surf was louder on the reefs. It would be hard to hear the motors of small boats tonight. There should have been a moon, but the night was impenetrably black, and wind and rain squalls swept the island.

It appears probable from the evidence developed since the war that the flashing lights were actually caused by the Japs firing a prelanding artillery preparation. The reason no shells landed on Wake is that they had made a gross error in navigation and all fire landed harmlessly in the ocean.

It was late before I was able to stretch out for a nap. Corporal Brown was on duty at the air raid warning phone, listening in on the network that was always kept open for simultaneous communications between all positions. It seemed to me I had hardly closed my eyes before Brown was calling me.

The enemy was reported landing on Toki Point. It was not quite 1:00 a.m., December 23.

"It came over the warning net," he said.

"Any confirmation?"

"No, sir."

But at each position, the Marine listening in on the network had heard the Toki Point report, and all over the island men were already scrambling in the dark to man battle stations.

I phoned Lieutenant Kessler: What about the report of a landing at Toki Point.

There were lights, he said. But no landing yet. Observers believed small boats were close off the north shore of Peale Island. He was manning beach defenses.

I told him, "That landing report came on the warning net. Check up and make sure."

While I was talking to Kessler, Lieutenant Poindexter called from his position near Camp One. He left a message that he had heard the report on the warning net; that he was taking off by truck with his "mobile reserve" to oppose the landing. He would have to pass my CP, so I ordered a man outside to stop the truck. My order for Poindexter was, "Stand by until the situation is clarified." Unless I had guessed entirely wrong, whatever was happening off Peale Island was at most a feint, and I didn't want Poindexter sucked out of the defense I had set up to meet the enemy's main attack. I still thought that the enemy would aim his heaviest blow at the beach between Peacock and Kuku points. That was the lee shore, in addition to everything else.

More reports were coming in: All batteries manned and ready. Machine guns manned along the shore. Such men as could be spared from gun crews were being deployed as infantry along the beaches. Small patrols— three or four men—were scouting the open sections of the long shoreline for signs of the enemy. They reported none except the lights north of the island.

Kessler was calling, "There are plenty of lights out there, but that's all."

"Any boats beached?"

"Negative."

I passed the word that the Toki Point landing was a false alarm. The enemy was there, all right, hidden by the darkness, probably in strong force, but he had not yet made his move. The enemy's continued failure to begin a preliminary bombardment and the opportunity for concealment offered him by the squally weather, made me more inclined to think his move might be a sneak landing, an attempt to slip ashore a landing force behind the curtain of darkness before we could discover what he was doing. In checking by phone with unit commanders, I stressed the need for extreme alertness, but no matter how alert a man may be or how much he may strain his eyes, he can't see through a wall. And the darkness around the island was a wall.

Then the enemy made his play.

At 1:15 a.m., "barges" were reported off Peacock Point. The "barges" were two destroyers, jam-packed with troops, but we didn't know that then. Then they were only darker blurs in the darkness.

Now reports were coming swiftly from all along the southern beach. Reports of "movement off shore." Reports of "some kind of craft close in." Whatever they were, they seemed to be moving in fast toward the beach.

At 1:20 a.m., machine guns on Wilkes Island opened fire.

Then everything started happening at once.

The Japs were coming ashore at four places. We had estimated correctly where they would hit, and now four landing groups were striking at that lee shore between Peacock and Kuku points.

The destroyers were heading for a spot about midway between Peacock Point and the west end of the airstrip. Between that spot and the channel, two landings were being made by troops in small boats. The fourth group was going in on Wilkes.

The Japanese plan for Wake proper was simple: the force from the destroyers would drive straight inland toward the airstrip. The next force down the beach would drive inland, turning the flank of any defenders attempting to hold up the main group. The third landing party, coming ashore near Camp One, would swing toward the channel, rolling back the Marines holding that part of the beach, preventing them from moving to aid the defenders of the airfield.

Some of the landing craft were beached and the Japs were already moving across the shore before they were discovered, before machine gun fire began breaking out in spots along that blacked-out strip of beach. The most lightly held sector of the southern beach was between the airfield and Camp One, and I ordered Lieutenant Poindexter to go there with his "mobile reserve" and take command of the defense.

When the destroyers were first sighted, they were so close in that the 5-inch guns on Peacock Point and Wilkes Island could not be brought to bear. The only gun which could bear on them was the 3-inch AA gun which Lieutenant Lewis had left for beach defense when his battery was shifted from its original position, days before. The gun, emplaced between the beach road and the airstrip, was close to the point for which the destroyers were racing in the dark, but we had no crew for it.

Lieutenant Hanna, commanding the .50 caliber machine guns at the airfield, volunteered to man the gun himself. He could spare only one man from his .50's, so the pair of them—the lieutenant and Corporal Ralph J. Holewinski—stumbled through the dark to man the gun by themselves. Three civilians saw what they were trying to do and volunteered to help them. Lieutenant Hanna did not take time to request permission before using them. The civilians were Bob Bryan, Paul Gay and Eric Lehtola. Paul Gay and Bob Bryan were subsequently killed in action and Eric Lehtola was wounded. Hanna later stated that they fought with "exceptional gallantry."

I could have ordered Lieutenant Lewis to send a crew to man the gun, and perhaps I should have done so, but I knew that daylight would bring the bombers and I wanted to hold Lewis' battery intact to oppose them. Except for machine guns, Lewis' guns were our only means of striking back at air attack.

I directed Major Putnam to place his aviation personnel as infantry between the 3-inch gun and the beach to protect Hanna while he fired. Major Putnam had Hank Elrod, Captain Tharin and perhaps twenty enlisted men.

I also pulled a squad from Godbold's battery, under Corporal Leon Graves, and when he reached my CP ordered him to proceed to Hanna's gun, but they never got there.

By the time Hanna reached the gun, the Japs were close aboard driving the destroyers straight into the reef. The first waves of Japanese were preparing to scramble off into the water, to wade ashore through pitch blackness and our almost blind machine gun fire.

Hanna's gun had no sights for him to use. The 3-inchers had electric repeaters for anti-aircraft fire, without sighting guides of any kind. These guns were developed by the Coast Artillery whose doctrine at the time did not, for some obscure reason, favor the employment of the gun in the direct fire role. Consequently, no sights were provided. Subsequently, some Marines corrected this obvious shortcoming with sights designed and built in the village blacksmith fashion. We had not, of course, had time to improvise any such sights. I remember that when I was a student officer at the Coast Artillery School I asked an instructor how fire would be conducted if the electronic fire control equipment were knocked out. His reply was to the effect that there was no alternate method.

It looked as though all Hanna could do was point the gun in the general direction of the enemy, but that was the best we could do. Hanna opened the breech of the gun and peered through the bore, adjusting the gun until by looking through the bore he could see his target, the blurred blobs of black in blackness that were the grounded destroyers.

"Okay," he said—and opened fire.

The first shell was a hit. Hanna kept firing as fast as he could load, pouring shells into the crowded destroyers, breaking fire only long enough to sight through the bore when he shifted targets. He blasted the vessels, made a slaughter pen of the crowded decks, and the destroyers burst into flame. Now the Marines could see the enemy. They could see Japs tumbling from the burning vessels into the water. The bonfire of the destroyers gave light enough for our machine gunners to sweep the crowded water, to pin down with fire the Japs who already had reached the shore.

Now the Marines were not fighting blindfolded. Now they could see something to shoot at. Now the fighting was general all along the shore—where the Japs were wading under Hanna's fire; where they were trying to push through Putnam's thin line to silence the gun; where Poindexter was fighting desperately to keep from being flanked. I had worked out data for beach barrages with Lewis days before, and now I ordered him to open fire.

To Pfc Wallace, watching from Peale Island, it looked like "a great big Fourth of July celebration." To the Japanese Navy Minister, Admiral Shimada, it was a battle "which would have made the gods weep." To the Japanese fighting on that beach, it was like this: —

It was 1 a.m. of December 23 when at last we received the order to make our forced landing . . . It was pitch dark. All we could see were stars twinkling in the sky and the waves breaking against our ves-

---

— This translation of a Japanese eyewitness account of the landing on Wake is quoted from *Japan Fights For Asia*, by John Goette, copyright, 1943, by Harcourt, Brace and Company, Inc. The Japanese writer apparently was on one of the destroyers set afire by Lieutenant Hanna.

sels. The enemy still seemed to be unaware of our presence.

Suddenly the voice of the ship's commander rang out in the ominous silence. "Shore ahead!" We all fell flat on the deck. With a loud crunching sound, the ship rode up on to the shore . . . . As we started to rise to our feet, the enemy opened fire all at once. Out of the darkness in front of us, shells came shrieking like a thousand demons let loose.

One shell exploded on the ship's bridge. Simultaneously several men fell where they stood. "Quick! Quick!" the excited voice of the commander could be heard above the uproar of combat.

Clambering down the ladders and ropes, we disembarked in great haste. But we were still not on land, as our ship had gone on a reef. The water was so deep we could hardly walk. Rifle in hand, we desperately fought our way forward.

Artillery shells, machine gun bullets, rifle bullets—the resisting fire of the enemy grew to a mad intensity. Lying flat on our faces on the beach at the edge of sea, we could not wriggle an inch.

The enemy's tracer bullets which came flying through the dark looked like a show of fireworks. The enemy's position seemed no farther than fifty yards away.

It was so dark that we could not fire even a single shot in reply. The enemy's fire grew increasingly intense. The bullets came flying very low. They pierced the gas masks on our backs in close succession. Little by little our gas masks were shot away.

Then the bullets began to pass close to our backs. But we could not move an inch. Time was passing all the while. We could not remain thus for much longer. It was either death or a charge at the enemy.

An inch at a time we crept toward the enemy. Twenty yards before the enemy, we prepared to charge. All at once a rain of hand grenades came hurtling down at us.

"Charge!" the commander's voice rang out. We jumped to our feet and charged. Huge shadows which shouted something unintelligible were pierced one after another. One large figure appeared before us to blaze away with a machine gun from his hip as they do in American gangster films. Somebody went for him with his bayonet and went down together with his victim.

That charge was against Putnam's detachment, and the Marines had to give ground. They fell back slowly, step by step, stubbornly contesting every foot of the ground, sometimes fighting hand-to-hand in the darkness, but they had to fall back. There were just too many Japs. By this time, the enemy had fully a thousand troops ashore on Wake proper. In the sparse, broken line opposing them were eighty-five Marines and perhaps fifteen civilians who fought without asking permission.

Meanwhile, Corporal Leon Graves had run into trouble. He commanded the squad I had pulled from Godbold's battery on Peale Island to reinforce Hanna at the start. The Japs were coming ashore by the time he got anywhere near the gun he was to man.

In that squad was Private Ralph Pickett. His mates

called him "Hezzie" because, according to one explanation, he "hesitated" to make Pfc. Young Private Pickett had been up for Pfc three or four times before we came to Wake, but each time he had celebrated his impending promotion so enthusiastically that he always lost his stripe before he actually got it. He finally gave up, with the philosophical comment, "I started as a private and I'll get paid off as a private."

I think it was Private Pickett who started the joke about the Jap list. He claimed the Japs had a list with everybody graded. A man who didn't hurt the Japs was way down the list; a man who caused them trouble was up near the top. When a gun crew would hit a bomber, Private Pickett would inform them gravely they they were no longer No. 32 on the Jap list. They were No. 14. Maybe it was pointless, but the weary men got a laugh out of it and the whole battery made the Jap list a running gag through the battle. Private Pickett was a good man for morale.

Now as Corporal Graves led them forward, Private Pickett drawled, "What we doing, Graves? Making numbers on the Jap list?"

Somebody laughed. Corporal Graves told them to knock it off. They went forward in silence. A Jap machine gun opened up. They hit the deck, forming a firing line, squeezing off their shots at the flashes in the dark. Pfc Sammy Jackson said Hezzie Pickett never knew what hit him. "He just let out a little groan and rolled on his side."

Somebody said Hezzie Pickett had finally made promotion: "Yeah, No. 1 on the Jap list." But that was later. Up there in the darkness, they were too busy for wisecracks. They fought doggedly, trying to push forward to Hanna's gun, trying to creep forward, but they couldn't. They were pinned down.

Meanwhile, as reports of the fighting poured in, as the reports began to give me a clearer picture of our problem, I ordered Major Potter to set up a secondary line with the CP personnel—clerks, communications men and everybody else except two enlisted men. I kept those two with me at the CP, one on the switchboard and the other on the warning net. Major Potter had about thirty men to form his line straddling the road a hundred yards below my CP. I chose that position because if the Japs broke through from the beach, part of their advance would have to be across the open airfield to reach Potter's line.

Potter's line was formed, at least partly, by the time Corporal Grave's squad had to fall back, unable to get through to Hanna's gun. They took their place in Potter's line.

While all this was happening, communications were breaking down. Just as the destroyers hit the reef, red flares had been observed. Small patrols were sent to search the lagoon shore, but they missed the enemy in the dark. We learned later that a number of Japanese had paddled into the lagoon in rubber boats and landed. Though we did not know it, they were behind us now, slipping about for a chance to snipe at us, searching for communications lines to cut. I do not know how much of our communications troubles were caused by these Japs or how much by mechanical failure, but the breaks in communications were a bitter handicap.

Communication with Wilkes was cut only a few minutes after the firing began. When Gunner McKinstry opened fire at the sound of the motor in the dark, Captain Platt requested permission to illuminate. Permission granted. A moment later, the searchlight on Wilkes lit up the beach. The searchlight had been badly damaged by bombing and now the light lasted less than a minute, but that was long enough to reveal a beached landing boat and Japs pouring ashore. A moment later, the telephone line from Wilkes went dead. We tried to raise them on the warning network, but there was no answer. Other positions reported heavy firing on

Wilkes. That was all we knew of what was happening there.

Now the enemy was shelling us with mortars and small guns from ships. Barninger reported machine gun fire was sweeping his position at Peacock Point but it was from a distance. There was no target on which his 5-inch guns could bear, but his crews were at the guns, crouching behind them for protection from the raking fire while they waited for a target. Barninger reported he was placing his range section with machine guns to hold the higher ground commanding his position. Then the line went dead.

West of the airfield, Poindexter's motley force of Marines, sailors and a few civilians was being pushed back toward the channel. The last word from Poindexter was that he was being flanked. Then there was only the sound of firing in the dark to tell us what was happening.

The swarming Japs surrounded Putnam's little band, but the Marines fought their way out of the ring. They fought their way back to Hanna's gun. Putnam was wounded, so weak from loss of blood that he would lose consciousness from time to time, but now he placed his men around the gun. He said, "This is as far as we go."

Six hours later, at the time of the surrender, his little group was still there.

The Japs came in a screaming rush. The night exploded in fire around the gun, and some of the Japs broke through, but they were cut down, and the Japanese wave broke on that little rock of men who could be killed but would not step back. The Japs tried to crawl in close to the position so they could blast it with grenades, but they were met with fire; sent scuttering back into the dark. Now the position was surrounded, now the Japs were blasting them from all directions, but still they hung on, hardly twenty men against the hundreds; still they held in the center of the

Japs' advance.

I didn't know what was happening to them. By this time, we had lost communication with all forward positions except Lewis' battery and a .50 caliber machine gun position just east of the airstrip. That position should have been commanded by at least a sergeant, but we were so shorthanded on Wake that Corporal Winford J. McAnally was in command. He had only six Marines and perhaps three or four civilians as the Japs poured in around him, but he acted like a man with an army.

McAnally still had communication with the machine guns north of Peacock Point as well as with my CP, and he kept reporting information from those positions as well as his own observations. That was about the only information I was getting as we tried vainly to restore communications with forward positions.

Corporal McAnally's position covered the road and he smashed a Jap attempt to advance along it. He took on himself the job of coordinating the fire of the machine guns north of Peacock, calling on them to fire or telling them to duck down because he was going to fire in their direction. He was closer to the Japs, in a better position to spot the enemy's movement in the dark, and he kept that area under such closely interlacing fire that the Japs could not push through.

The enemy spotted his position and tried to rush it. McAnally's crew beat them off. The enemy tried to crawl close enough for a grenade blast and a quick rush, but McAnally heard them. He held his fire until he couldn't miss—and then opened up with the machine gun and all the rifles he had.

But the Japs kept trying, and each time they drew closer; each time they were a little nearer to surrounding him. Once they did, it was all up with McAnally and his men. He called me for reinforcements.

"Sir, we got to have some help if we're going to hold this."

I had nobody to send. I told him he could withdraw.

"Well, sir," he said, "I reckon we can make out a little longer."

And he kept on fighting.

I was tempted to leave the CP and try to find out for myself what was happening. In a dugout, with communications crippled, with a thousand questions and no answers, you feel like a blindfolded man in a prize fight. Perhaps I should have made a personal reconnaissance, but Major Potter was out there setting up the secondary line and it seemed to me I had to stay where I was. There was not much I could learn wandering around in the dark, and the CP was where information came and control centered. It was where the officers would call for orders. So there I stuck, most of the time with a phone at each ear, trying to get through to the forward positions; trying to evaluate the information that dribbled back from McAnally, from Lewis, from Potter; trying to estimate what was happening out there in the dark.

According to field manual practice, I should have been able, when wire communication failed, to switch to voice radio. In fact, such radio equipment as was available on Wake had never functioned satisfactorily, and when most needed we did not have an effective radio network. The only tactical radios we had were unreliable "walkie talkie" hand sets.

Godbold and Kessler reported all quiet on Peale; only occasional lights off shore. I ordered Godbold to form his battery and .50 caliber personnel as infantry and proceed by truck to my CP. I did not now believe the enemy would attempt a landing on that windward side of the island. If they did, Kessler would just have to do the best he could. It was a risk I had to take to build up the secondary line that was our only chance of stopping the Japs if they broke through at the airfield.

Lewis reported mortar shells were falling on the air-

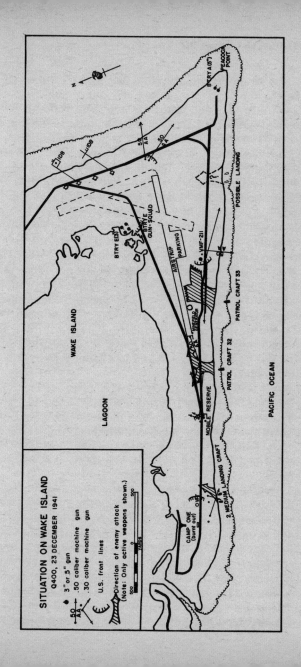

SITUATION ON WAKE ISLAND
Q400, 23 DECEMBER 1941

⊡ 3" or 5" gun
50 / AA — .50 caliber machine gun
.30 caliber machine gun
U.S. front lines
Direction of enemy attack
(Note: Only active weapons shown.)

500   0   500
        YARDS

WAKE ISLAND

LAGOON

PACIFIC OCEAN

CAMP ONE (burnt out)

2 MEDIUM LANDING CRAFT

MOBILE RESERVE

PATROL CRAFT 32

PATROL CRAFT 33

PATROL CRAFT

VMF-211

AIRSTRIP PARKING

GUN SQUAD

BTRY E (5")

BTRY A(5")

PEACOCK POINT

5" AA

108

field and that he was receiving rifle fire in his position. He requested permission to send out a gun crew as infantry to cover his battery. Permission granted. Sergeant Gragg's crew pushed out, but they were pinned down by enemy fire within fifty yards of the position.

Did that mean the enemy had broken through? Or was it only sniper fire? The intensity of the fire beyond the airfield, dwindling at times but always flaring up again, made me think that Putnam was still holding out. But I didn't know. A reconnaissance patrol sent out could not get through. I didn't know what was happening on Wilkes. Or what had happened to Poindexter after the last report that he was being flanked.

And what about Kliewer? If the Japs captured the airstrip, he was supposed to blow it up. The runway was mined with dynamite, and Lieutenant Kliewer had been assigned with three men to a generator near the west end of the strip to explode the dynamite if the time came. There had been fighting at that end of the field, but there had been no word from Kliewer. We couldn't contact him.

A wild-eyed civilian staggered in. He had been cut off when the Japs pushed Poindexter back. He had been playing hide-and-seek for his life in the dark and he didn't know what had happened to Poindexter. He said he saw the Japs knock out the machine guns west of the airfield. He said he saw the Japs bayonet the crews.

"They're killing 'em all," he said.

I tried to question him, but he was too shaken to tell much. He kept repeating that he had seen the Japanese stabbing men at the guns. There was still fighting down there, but maybe it was only the Japs mopping up the last isolated pockets of resistance. I tried to calculate the accuracy of the civilian's information. He was on the verge of collapse from fear and exhaustion, but he stuck to his story of what he said he'd seen. It was the first news we'd had of the battle west of the airport since the lines went dead, and there was no reason to doubt his story. I looked at my watch. It would be getting light in a little while. I was wondering how long it would take Godbold's men to arrive when Corporal Brown broke in.

"I've got something, sir." He was listening on the warning network. Somebody was whispering into one of the phones on the network. The voice kept whispering the same thing over and over:

"There are Japanese in the bushes . . . . There are definitely Japanese in the bushes . . . . "

Brown said, "Who's this? Where are you?" But the voice kept whispering:

"There are Japanese in the bushes . . . . "

At other positions men were listening to the whispering on the network and one of them blurted, "For Christ's sake, where are you?"

The only answer was the whisper: "There are Japanese in the bushes . . . . "

It was like hearing a dead man talk. He was speaking so carefully, so monotonously, over and over, every now and then repeating that word "definitely." Brown kept asking him who he was, where he was, but the whisperer's power of reception must have been gone. He could not even know that anyone was hearing his message. He could only whisper into a telephone, somewhere in the dark.

Trying to warn us before they got him. Trying to warn us before he died. But not remembering we could not tell on the network where he was calling from.

"There are definitely Japanese . . . . "

There was a burst of sound, and Corporal Brown could not tell afterward whether it was a scream, but the whispering stopped.

"I guess they got him," Brown said.

In a little while, it would be day.

Chater Twelve

"The Men from Mars"

THE LAST I HAD HEARD FROM Lieutenant Poindexter before communications failed was that he was being flanked; that he was falling back toward the channel. The only word after that was the fleeing civilian's report that the Japs had overrun Poindexter's machine guns and slaughtered the crews. This is what really happened to Poindexter's "mobile reserve," though I did not learn it until after the surrender.

When I sent Lieutenant Poindexter back to the south beach from my CP, the destroyers were close enough to be seen racing toward the island and his beach positions reported "something" moving toward their sector of the shore. Then the machine guns on Wilkes opened fire. A few moments later, one of Poindexter's guns began firing at dark shapes sliding out of the night. Landing craft were coming ashore there, spilling troops onto the beach.

Most of Poindexter's men—Marines, hastily armed bluejackets and a few civilians—had been strung out thinly in order to cover his section of the beach, from the channel eastward toward the airfield. So now he lacked sufficient fire power concentrated at that focal point to stop the enemy coming ashore. Poindexter ran down to the beach, going forward himself to hurl grenades among the enemy, trying to organize stronger resistance at the landing point. The Marines from his truck followed as he tried to build up a line strong enough to hold the enemy, but it was hard in the confusion of fire and darkness, and at first men were mostly fighting on their own.

In the brush, watching flame splash the night, hearing the shouts of fighting men he could not see, a civilian crouched. I will call him "Pop." He had fought in France as a lieutenant. Then he had married, found pride in his sons and success in business, and the world was a good place. He had been an executive for a big corporation and still going up the ladder when liquor threw him. He lost his job and the next one wasn't so good. He slipped down the ladder, each job worse than the one before, until it hardly seemed worth the bother to get another job.

His wife couldn't take it any longer. She divorced him and took the children. After that, he wandered around the country, working when he had to at any job he could get, then bumming on as soon as he got a few bucks, just wandering from binge to binge until he heard about Wake Island and decided a job at a place like that was his last chance to save himself.

He was grey, getting bald, when he came to Wake as a dishwasher, the executive turned "pot-walloper," but by the time war began Pop had worked up to a job in the office. Now he was in the brush and they were fighting on the beach. Maybe he remembered something then, something he had forgotten for years. Or maybe not. He didn't say. He crawled to a Marine emplacement and groped in the dark until he found a box of grenades. He took as many as he could carry and started running toward the enemy.

Bullets were spattering the sand where he ran, but he kept on, stumbling a little, running toward a shadow moving in the night. Another landing boat was coming in. He was wading in the water now, but he kept on until he was close enough to lob grenades into the crowded boat as it grated on the sand. There was a lot of yelling, screaming, as the Japs tried to scramble off, but Pop stood there in the water tossing grenades among them until he was empty-handed.

He went back for more grenades, but by this time the enemy was ashore in force from the other landing boats; by this time the fight was moving up the shore as the Japs tried to push through to the channel. Pop took his place in the line.

The Japanese pressed their attack methodically. They had pushed inland to the road, before they swung to drive toward the channel. They kept pushing detachments farther inland, trying to turn Poindexter's flank, and he had to pull slowly back. He did not have the men to extend his line. He could not see what was happening in the dark. His odds-and-ends detachment was heavily outnumbered and fighting blind, trying to stop an enemy they could not see. Men could fire only at flashes or the empty dark or wait until shadows loomed up before them, sometimes almost close enough to touch. They were helped by the light from the burning destroyers down the beach, but mostly it was a battle in the dark. They fought all the way. They fought on the beach and in the brush and on the road, but they had to keep falling back to escape being flanked in the dark.

Then the darkness was fading. Men were beginning to see. Sergeant Elwood Smith reported Japanese on the lagoon side. There were only a few, probably landed from the rubber boats, but now they were prowling around trying to pick off Marines behind the firing line.

A civilian named Gordon had sought shelter behind a chunk of coral. In the dim early light, a couple of these Japs spotted him. They began shooting at him. Mr. Gordon was clutching a grenade he had picked up, but he discreetly hugged the deck behind his chunk of coral. Mr. Gordon was a large man, however, and the lump of coral was not big enough to hide all of him.

The Japs could still see his bottom sticking up. They kept firing at it, the bullets splattering into the sand beside him, until Mr. Gordon got angry. He raised up and threw his grenade. They say his form was lamentably unregulation, but the grenade landed between the two Japanese. They didn't do any more shooting at anybody.

Meanwhile, as he fell back, Poindexter had been picking up men and now others were able to see what was around them and make their way to join him. Sergeant Smith scraped together the last available men and moved up to the line. Poindexter now had some seventy Marines and sailors. He said they'd do the shoving for a change. The Japs came on, but Poindexter was through retreating. He started forward. It was a dirty, bitter job, but they slowly fought their way back along the way they had come, pushing the enemy back toward the airfield.

But at the CP, we did not know this. Nor did we know what had happened to Lieutenant Kliewer and his detail assigned to blow up the airstrip if the time came.

The generator with which they were to explode the buried dynamite was at the west end of the runway. With Kliewer were Staff Sergeant J.F. Blandy and Sergeants R.E. Bourquin, Jr., and C.E. Trego. They were armed with two tommyguns, three pistols and two boxes of grenades. The Japanese moving in from the beach stumbled on them and were beaten off. By 2:00 a.m. their communications lines was cut and the Japs were surrounding them.

The Japs tried a bayonet charge, but it was blasted with tommygun fire and grenades. Several times the Japs tried to rush them in the dark, but each time the four Marines beat off the attack. In the lulls between attacks, they discussed whether they should blow up the field now and escape in the dark, but Lieutenant Kliewer said the orders were to blow it up only to keep the Japs from getting it. Their job was to hang on until they knew that was about to happen.

As the morning grew dimly light, the Japs made a concentrated attack. This time they were determined to sweep over the four men who had held them up for hours. The Marines were firing as fast as they could, flinging grenades into the face of the charge, but there were too many Japs. This is it. This was the finish.

But at the west end of the airfield, 150 yards or so away, a machine gun crew was able to see the Japs in the early light. They caught the Japs with .50 caliber fire. It was like a sickle through grass. The charge ended in thickly scattered dead.

As it grew lighter, Kliewer was able to see Jap flags all along the shore. He could see Jap flags at numerous places farther inland, too. He decided it was time to blow up the airstrip.

"We'll set her off and then retreat to that .50 caliber position behind us," he said.

But the intermittent rain through the night had drowned the mechanism. And the Japs were attacking again. The .50 caliber gun again helped them beat off the attack, and then they worked on the generator, trying to get it started so they could explode the buried dynamite. They had to interrupt their work from time to time when Japs crawled too near or tried to rush them. They were almost surrounded now. If they waited much longer they wouldn't be able to retreat anywhere. But they kept working on the motor.

That was about the time Corporal McAnally met the "men from Mars" at the east end of the airstrip.

The Marine who saw them first said, "What the hell's that?"

McAnally looked at the two figures moving out of the brush. They had strange eyes and weird tanks on their back.

"Looks like men from Mars," he said—and opened fire.

One of the weird-looking men dropped for cover behind a big chunk of coral, but the other was killed. He flopped with his feet sticking up. It looked as though he had webbed feet, but that was only the split-toed Jap shoes. The men from Mars were Japanese wearing big goggles and armed with flame throwers. They had been sent to burn out the positions still holding up the advance.

The Jap behind the big chunk of coral must have felt pretty safe, but Corporal McAnally sighted his machine gun on the center of the chunk and opened fire. The stream of bullets chipped through the coral like an ice pick. When the lump was chipped through, the hiding Jap got the bullets. So, they never did get the chance to use the flame throwers.

But all of this, of all that was happening from the airstrip to the sea, the only word I had was Corporal McAnally's report that he had killed Japanese armed with flame throwers.

Over on Peale Island, Pfc Wallace couldn't forget that he might still have been in Philadelphia if he'd kept his mouth shut when he had a few beers with his pal. He and Pfc Albert Breckenridge had been watching the fireworks of battle from their posts on the shore of the lagoon. It must have been quite a show from where they sat. Pfc Wallace remembered later that Pfc Breckenridge even forgot to boast about Dallas and Texas. He was rather thoughtful.

"I bet we never see the sun rise," he said.

Pfc Wallace said, "Nuts."

Then they climbed into trucks with the rest of Godbold's men to move to Wake. It was getting light when the last of them reached my CP. They climbed from the trucks and moved forward afoot to fill in Potter's line. I had finally been forced to withdraw Corporal McAnally's crew from the airstrip to save them from being cut off, and now Potter's line was beginning to receive scattered fire.

Breckenridge and Wallace were digging in as day

came. Wallace stopped digging.

"You lost that bet," he said. "There's the sunrise."

Breckenridge was not convinced. He said, "Well, I bet we never see it set."

From his own hole, Pfc Verga heard the discussion. He also heard a bullet whine past them and yelled:

"Get down, you dopes! That ain't no humming-bird!"

They finished their holes from the inside, and by that time the enemy was appearing on the other side of the strip. By that time, Potter's men were getting something to shoot at.

In the brush near Lewis' battery, under sniper fire as they waited to defend the guns, Shorty Martin looked at Sergeant Gragg as the day came. The snipers were hitting closer, but Pfc Martin sounded as cheerful as ever:

"Good morning, Sergeant Gragg! I sincerely hope I can say the same thing tomorrow morning."

About then, dive bombers were sighted approaching the island. As they approached in formation, six thousand feet or more in the air, Lewis' battery engaged them until the formation split and the Japs went into their bombing glides.

Now it was light enough to see the Japanese fleet. It lay in a vast circle around the island, surrounding us, but far out of range of any gun we had. Men tried to count the ships—it was like counting their own chances of staying alive another day—but even now we do not know exactly the strength of that Japanese fleet. Major Potter reported sixteen men-of-war, light and heavy cruisers. Lieutenant Barninger counted twenty-seven ships of all kinds, and some of the enlisted men thought there were more. Lieutenant Kessler reported at least four of the Japanese vessels were battleships or "super-cruisers." But whatever force the enemy had in that far, slow moving circle, it was more than enough and every man of us knew it. At any moment the enemy wished, whenever they got the word from the Japs ashore so they would not kill their own men, their big guns could blow us out of the sea—and at that range our heaviest batteries were as useless as BB rifles.

Then Kessler was calling from Toki Point. Jap ships were in range: three destroyers closing in off Wilkes. He opened on the lead destroyer with both 5-inch guns. The fourth salvo got her. She swerved sharply, badly hit. Kessler shifted fire to the next target, but the undamaged Japs escaped by running away. The wounded destroyer also tried to flee, but Marines watching from the shore reported that she sank. From the study of all evidence available after the war it is impossible to completely substantiate the claim—nor is it possible to refute it. The fact is, we will never know for sure.

After that, the Jap ships discreetly remained out of range until after the surrender. We learned later that some of them thought we had 16-inch guns on the island, which was rather a compliment to the Marines manning our 5-inch batteries.

Commander Cunningham left the conduct of the battle to me, but I was in constant touch by telephone with his CP dugout in the direction of Camp Two, reporting developments as I learned them through the hours of blind fighting in the dark. Now, about 7:00 a.m., I reported to Commander Cunningham the way the situation looked from my CP. We had no communication with Wilkes Island or any other forward positon, so my estimate of the situation had to be based largely on guesswork and probabilities.

This was how it seemed to me:

Jap flags were reported flying "all over Wilkes." In the absence of any indication to the contrary, I had to assume that Wilkes Island had fallen.

On Wake proper, all along the front of the Japanese advance, the enemy had pushed through to the airstrip and even beyond. The firing line set up by Major Potter—our secondary line—lay across the road only one hundred yards below my CP and now it was our first line. Now some of Potter's men were firing on the advancing Japs at three hundred yards or less. The enemy's return fire at that range was from light machine guns as well as rifles, and the Marines could see increasing forward movement all along the enemy's front.

Major Potter had tried to close the gap between the right flank of his line and Lewis' 3-inch battery position on the lagoon side, but he could spare only a squad from his starvation-thin line for the attempt and the squad he sent to plug the hole was driven back after losing two men. Now Gunner Hamas reported that Potter's right flank was receiving fire from the lagoon side as well as from the front. And in the concealing brush on the lagoon side, in the crook of the horseshoe, Sergeant Gragg's crew defending Lewis' battery as infantry were still unable to push out far enough to prevent enemy rifle fire into Lewis' position. Gragg's crew were still pinned down by unseen Jap fire near the battery.

By this time, Lieutenant Kliewer's detail should have blown up the airstrip and the demolition volunteer at the boat channel should long since have exploded his dynamite-laden barge to block the channel, but there had been no explosion and now the enemy was well past both positons.

From all this, I had to assume that our forward positions had been overrun or, at best, broken up and isolated in a few helpless "last stand" pockets that could do us no good. I had to report to Commander Cunningham that it looked to me as though the Japs had secured Wilkes Island, Camp One, the channel, the airstrip and probably Barninger's positon as well, and that now the enemy was eating his way into the island with Potter's line as the next bite.

I said, "That's the best I can judge the picture on the dope I've got."

There was a long moment before he replied. Then:

"Well, I guess we'd better give it to them."

I could not believe he had said it. I had not contemplated even the possibility of surrender. If we could not hold the enemy at Potter's line, we could fall back and try again at another position, even though that probably would mean pulling over Kessler's battery as infantry, leaving Peale Island naked to a landing. I do not think any of us had thought further than trying to hold the enemy as long as possible at each position, buying time, for next day ships were scheduled to evacuate the civilians and we all felt sure those ships were part of a task force bringing reinforcements.

But now he was saying we had to surrender.

I said, "Isn't any help coming?"

"No," he said. "There are no friendly ships within twenty-four hours."

"Not even submarines?"

"Not even them."

I said, "Let me see if there isn't something I can do up here."

He didn't reply at once. I knew now he was considering the lives of the unarmed civilians, more than a thousand lives for which he was responsible. Then, quietly:

"All right, Jim."

I told him I needed riflemen desperately and I could not strip Peale except as a last-stand resort, but Commander Cunningham didn't have any to send me. The only riflemen guarding his CP were the five Army communications men I had armed when war began. Five men would not have helped much.

I tried to think of something—anything—we might do to keep going, but there wasn't anything. Even if we could stop the advance temporarily, even if we killed every Jap on the island, the enemy had only to pour ashore more men and still more until we were swamped. He had only to sit off there with his fleet in perfect safety and blast the island until his men could stroll ashore. And their dive bombers were still attacking. It was a numbing realization, bitter to take, but Commander Cunningham's decision to surrender was inevitable, beyond argument. We could keep on spending lives, but we could not buy anything with them.

So I said, "I'll pass the word."

I got up to do what I had to do as Gunner Hamas came in. He reported the last of Godbold's men had arrived on the line. What were my orders now?

I said, "It's too late, John. Commander Cunningham has ordered us to surrender. Fix up a white flag and pass the word to cease firing."

He looked at me as though I were crazy. John Hamas born in Zemplin-Humenne, in what became Czechoslovakia, was a veteran of World War I. He had served in the Austro-Hungarian army and won his commission as lieutenant in the Czech infantry before enlisting in the Marines in 1921. He had been a Marine ever since, serving over the world, the kind of legendary character that men write stories about. He did such a job of fighting in Nicaragua that the President of the Republic offered him a colonel's commission if he would stay when the Marines pulled out. The pay was $900 a month, a giddy fortune to a sergeant of Marines, but Sergeant Hamas turned it down. As he put it, "They might change presidents on me in Nicaragua, but a Marine is sure of his pension." Now he had to pass the order for Marines to surrender. I think his reply to me was probably the hardest thing John Hamas ever made himself do. He said, "Yes, sir."

He went out, and from the doorway of the dugout I heard him shouting the order to cease fire. He sounded like a kid who was trying not to blubber.

"Major's orders! We're surrendering . . . . Major's orders . . . . "

I was told a long time later that I stepped to the

entrance and yelled at him, "It's not my order, God damn it!"

Maybe I did, but I don't remember it. A lot of men must have forgotten things they said in that numbed time it took us to realize this was actually happening to us, this death of pride.

I was giving the word to all positions I could reach by phone when a call from Barninger's battery came through. They had managed to repair the line at last. They still held their position, ready for attack. What were my orders? It was too late for anything except to repeat the word:

> Cease firing. Destroy all weapons. The
> island is being surrendered.

Along Potter's scattered line, the order was passed from man to man, but some of them off in the brush didn't get the word and some wouldn't believe it when they did. They kept fighting on their own, mostly alone, one man with a rifle trying for one more shot at the enemy before they got him.

A corporal crawling along the line brought the news to Pfc Breckenridge and his pal, Pfc Wallace. Breckenridge had lost his bet that they would never see the sun rise and then he had bet they would never see it set. Now Wallace said, "Breck, I guess you're going to win that second bet."

They took the bolts from their rifles and flung them as far off into the brush as they could. If the Japs wanted to use those rifles, they'd have to do some hunting first.

They sat down to wait for the Japs to come for them. Pfc Wallace remembers he took out the letter he had carried through the battle, the letter from his girl in Pennsylvania telling him how happy she was that he was in the Pacific where he would not be in danger. He slowly tore it into little pieces and let them blow out of his hand. Neither of them said anything as they sat watching the tiny bits of paper scatter over the sand.

At the artillery positions, blankets were stuffed into the muzzles of the guns and the guns were fired. To make sure the enemy could never repair the damaged guns, Marines then dropped grenades into the muzzles. They cut all cables, broke gun dials, destroyed the firing locks. Lieutenant Lewis' battery used twenty pistol shots to make sure their director and height-finder were damaged beyond repair. Sergeant Robert Box was firing his .45 into the height-finder when a bullet ricocheted and hit him. He turned the air blue with his comments on the luck that would bring a man through a battle—and let him wound himself when it was over.

When their weapons and equipment were wrecked, the Marines on Peale Island and Peacock Point sat down to gorge themselves, to eat up as much as they could of their food supply before the Japs came for them. There was no sense saving food now and it might be their last meal.

About forty minutes after the first word to surrender had been given, Lieutenant Lewis marched his men to the CP and reported:

"Sir, the guns and fire control equipment of E Battery have been destroyed."

He kept his tired, streaked face expressionless, but his men stood staring at the white flag over the CP—a bedsheet nailed to a timber—and there was bewilderment and resentment in their faces. They could hear firing up ahead, the fight was still going on, and they had been ordered to destroy their guns and quit.

I told them, "I don't know whether any Marines have ever surrendered before, but those are the orders and they'll be carried out."

As they relaxed, sitting down to wait for the Japs or sprawling wearily on the ground, somebody asked what the Japs would do with them.

Sergeant Gragg said, "If they don't shoot us, we'll

probably go to Manchukuo and work in the salt mines."

A Pfc drawled, "Join the Marines and see the world—the hard way."

Somebody laughed. Somebody broke out a small supply of hoarded chocolate bars. They had to break the bars in half to make them go around, but there was no use saving them now. So they waited, munching candy, for the Japs to come.

Meanwhile, Platoon Sergeant Bernard Ketner came to the CP on an errand from the firing line. He must have stood watching me as I worked at the phone, but I did not notice him until he stepped up to me and stuck out his hand.

He said, "Don't worry, Major. You fought a good fight and did all you could."

We shook hands, and then the sergeant trudged back to the line and I picked up the telephone again.

I knew the enemy's advance units were near the military hospital, which was between my CP and the enemy. (My CP was the third of four underground magazines lying along the road in a line at right angles to the airfield and east of it. The military hospital occupied the first magazine in this line while the second was used for bomb storage and the fourth as the civilian hospital. The first and fourth magazines were used as hospitals because they were the only ones empty when the hospital had to be moved underground after the December 9 raid. I did not move my CP to a magazine until the night of December 14-15.)

I had called Dr. Kahn, the Navy doctor, to raise a white flag and give word of the surrender to a Jap officer, if he could manage contact with one. Now my phone man turned from the switchboard:

"Sir, the hospital doesn't answer."

I spoke to a group, "Rig a white flag you can carry. We'll have to go down there."

A sergeant, Donald Malleck, volunteered and tied a white rag on a swab handle and the two of us started walking down the road toward the enemy.

We didn't know it, but the Japs already had captured the hospital. They celebrated the capture by firing into the crowded dugout, killing a civilian and wounding a naval officer. Then they herded the sick and wounded out of the hospital and prodded them into lines along the road.

Before Sergeant Malleck and I reached the hospital, we met the Japanese point, the leading man of their advance. We stopped in the middle of the road and Sergeant Malleck held up his white flag. The Jap came toward us with slow caution, covering us with his rifle, finger on the trigger. He stopped a few feet from us, his fixed bayonet ready to lunge, and peered at us. He could not help seeing the insignia of my rank on my shirt collar.

He motioned with his bayonet, making me understand I must drop my helmet and pistol belt and empty my pockets on the ground. He let me keep my handkerchief and wallet; nothing else.

He made Malleck do the same. He even made Malleck take off his shirt and leave it on the ground. Then he stepped aside and motioned with his bayonet for us to precede him toward the Jap lines. He followed a few paces behind us.

We had gone only a few steps when we saw the second man of the Jap advance party waiting in the road. As we approached him, a rifle cracked in the brush. The Jap fell on his face.

I yelled, "The order has been given to cease firing, and damn it, you'll obey that order!"

The shot must have been fired by one of Potter's men who failed to get the word and failed to see our white flag in the brush. Our guard only motioned us to walk on to the fallen man. He stooped and rolled the body over. He saw the man was dead, but he showed neither pity nor anger. He simply motioned for us to move on.

The Japs had cleared the hospital when we reached it. There were about thirty Americans—wounded, sick and ablebodied—and all had been stripped down to their skivvies and shoes. Now they sat in four rows beside the road with eight machine guns at their backs. Their hands were lashed behind them with telephone wire and one end of the wire was noosed around each man's neck. If he tried to free his hands or even ease the strain of the wire cutting into his wrists, he would tighten the noose around his neck.

Several Japanese were standing at the hospital door, watching us approach. One of them was wearing a sword, so I knew he was an officer. I asked him, "Do you speak English?"

"Yes, a ritter."

"Well, we are surrendering."

His face lit up. He said something to his men and then gave me a cigarette. He was trying to act nonchalant, but I think he was only trying to hide his fear that our surrender was a trick.

I asked, "Where did you learn English?"

"Studied at schoor. A'so, was at San Francisco Wor'd Fair, 1939."

Somebody yelled excitedly, and we saw that a Japanese sentry had stopped one of our trucks. Commander Cunningham got out and walked toward us. I was surprised to see he had changed to his formal blue uniform. The Jap officer—a Navy lieutenant, junior grade—looked from Cunningham to me undecidedly.

"Who Number One?" he asked.

I pointed to Cunningham. I said that while he arranged the formal surrender, I would go around the island with Malleck to be sure that everybody got the word to surrender. The World's Fair jg and about twenty troops escorted us back to the CP where I made sure that all our men in the vicinity were disarmed. Then we started walking toward Camp One.

As we crossed the airstrip, we met the commander of

the Jap landing force, a Navy captain. He had been wounded in the hand. He shook his head when I asked if he spoke English, but he handed me a pad and pencil. I knew many Japanese can read and write English without speaking it, so I scribbled: "I will stop the fighting." I left further explanation to the World's Fair jg.

Another Jap jg joined our party as we started on. I made the usual inquiry: Did he speak English? In perfect English, he replied:

"No, I do not speak English. Do you speak Japanese?"

He walked directly behind me. He kept swinging his sword as though anxious to use it.

It was about 9:30 a.m., seven hours since I had lost communication with my forward positions. Now we came to Hanna's gun, the 3-inch gun he had volunteered to man for beach defense when the enemy started landing.

When Major Putnam's sparse line defending the gun was broken by the irresistible force of numbers, thirteen Marines and civilians rallied around Hanna's gun for a last stand. They were surrounded. The enemy swept the position with heavy fire. From the safe shelter of revetments built for our planes, the Japs dropped a pounding rain of rifle grenades on the defenders. Three of the thirteen defenders of the gun were killed and nine were wounded. Only Captain Tharin was still unhit, but he and the nine wounded men were still holding at bay at least two hundred Japanese when I climbed onto a revetment and yelled to them.

"This is Major Devereux! The island has been surrendered! Cease firing! Put down your weapons!"

There was no answer.

I shouted again and walked closer. Our men could see me now. I walked closer, calling that the island had surrendered. Now a few of them were coming out to meet me. Major Putnam looked like hell itself. He had been shot in the jaw. His face was a red smear.

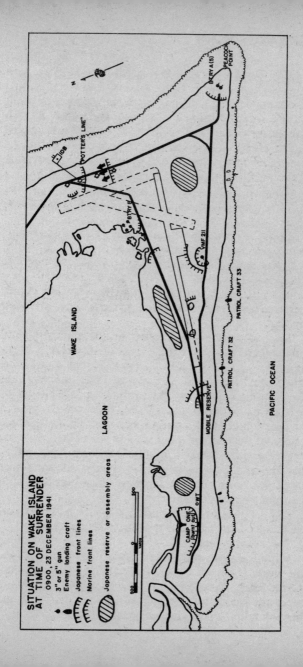

SITUATION ON WAKE ISLAND
AT TIME OF SURRENDER
0900, 23 DECEMBER 1941

3" or 5" gun
Enemy landing craft
Japanese front lines
Marine front lines
Japanese reserve or assembly areas

YARDS
500   0   500

WAKE ISLAND

LAGOON

"POTTER'S LINE"

1008

BTRY E

VMF 211

MOBILE RESERVE

CAMP ONE
(burnt out)

WT

BTRY A (5)
PEACOCK POINT

PATROL CRAFT 32

PATROL CRAFT 33

PACIFIC OCEAN

He said, "Jimmy, I'm sorry, poor Hank is dead."

Elrod had been a fury. Men remember how one charge almost overwhelmed them and how Hank Elrod stood upright, blasting with a tommygun and broke the charge. Japs fell that time close enough for him to touch. A man remembers Elrod saying, "Kill the sons-a-bitches!" They remember he was standing up to throw a grenade when a Jap shot him. The Jap had crawled in among the enemy dead scattered thickly around the position and waited there for his chance. Somebody killed the Jap, but Elrod never knew it. He died instantly. Now he lay there with his eyes open, defiant, and the grenade still tightly clutched in his hand. With him at the gun died Robert Bryan and Paul Gay, civilian volunteers.

The Japs separated Major Putnam, Captain Tharin and Lieutenant Hanna from the men and left both groups under guard while the rest of us walked on toward Camp One.

We stumbled on another siege at the generator pit where Lieutenant Kliewer and his three sergeants were still trying to blow up the airstrip. The four Marines were still alternately beating off Jap attacks and working on their stalled generator, trying to get it started so they could explode the dynamite buried under the strip.

They held their fire when they saw me approaching with Malleck and the white flag. The Japs were a little behind us. I stopped and called to them that the island had been surrendered.

One of the sergeants grabbed Kliewer's arm. "Don't surrender, Lieutenant! It's a hoax. Marines never surrender."

But finally Kliewer shook his head and stood wearily up. The escort party took Kliewer's detail under guard and we went on. It occurred to me to thank God in my heart that Kliewer had not succeeded in blowing up the airstrip while we were crossing it. Even if we had escaped the explosion, the Japs would have murdered us all for what they would have considered an act of treachery.

We gathered in the crews of two .50 caliber machine guns still holding out at the end of the airfield and then pushed on toward the sound of small arms fire in the direction of Camp One.

We came up behind fifty or sixty Japanese in a fire fight with troops we could not see. The Japs were getting the worst of it. They were giving ground when they saw us. Our white flag was flying plainly, but some of the Japs swung around and fired at us. A bunch of them—a couple of dozen maybe—charged us with bayonets.

The sword-swinging jg stepped forward, shouting at them until they stopped the charge, but then he let them jostle us around, pushing and pulling us, making us turn out our pockets. They didn't seem to want anything we had, not even as a souvenir. They just thumbed through our things and threw them away, money and everything else, among the rest my wallet containing my only photograph of my wife and my son.

Now we could see the Marines who were pushing back the Japs: Poindexter and perhaps twenty of his "reserve." Poindexter's idea had been to fight his way back toward the airfield, driving the Japs before him, until he could hit the flank of the main Jap force driving inland toward the CP. Now he saw us standing there with the white flag and a bunch of Japs. He was grinning as he came down the road. He thought the Japs were our prisoners. The truth seemed to stun him. His reaction was like that of many men I have seen under emotion too strong for expression in any words.

He snapped his fingers and said, "Oh, shucks!"

We marched on, picking up prisoners in driblets. The guards were making us walk with our hands in the air, but the World's Fair jg told us, "Put them down." When he dropped back to the rear of the column, a guard rapped me sharply with his bayonet and motioned for me to put up my hands again. I obeyed, but the jg came back and told me to put them down. He and the guard argued back and forth, countermanding each other, while I wondered if this example of discipline was typical of the Japanese military. It was.

Our flag was still flying from the water tower at Camp One where we had hoisted the colors when the flagpole was shot down. When the Japs saw the flag, some of them broke into a run, cheering and yelling, and one of the Japs began climbing the tower. I looked at my men. They were staring at the Japs with burning eyes. Fists were clenching. They were at the breaking point, the crazy point where a man will go against a gun with bare hands.

I snapped, "Hold it! Keep your heads, all of you!"

They could only get themselves killed if they tried to stop the Japs. So we stood watching while the grinning Jap on the tower cut our colors down, stuffed them in a camouflage net and climbed back to the ground with his prize.

Platoon Sergeant Dave J. Rush did not know about the surrender when he caught sight of the Jap climbing the water tower to cut down the flag. Sergeant Rush told me later that he drew a perfect bead with a machine gun, on the climbing Jap, but fortunately held his fire for a few seconds—and then saw the surrender party. Otherwise, it would have been extremely embarrassing to us.

Gunnery Sergeant Jon Cemeris was at a .30 caliber machine gun near the small boat channel and didn't see us, either, but he did see a Jap dive bomber swooping in. Cemeris opened up with his gun. A .30 caliber is normally used for ground defense, but Cemeris bagged the Jap. I saw the Jap jettison his bombs and later we learned that the plane crashed. It was beautiful shooting, but it made things a little ticklish for us because our Jap escort also saw it, but they only prodded us on to the small boat channel.

I had been unable to order the dynamite-laden barge blown up in the channel after communications failed and the civilian volunteer assigned to the éxploder had been unwilling to assume the responsibility of destroying the channel without orders. I told the sword-swinging lieutenant about the dynamite barge. Nothing could be gained now by trying to hide it and an accidental explosion might cause the Japs to massacre us.

I thought our job was finished when we reached the channel, but the sword-swinger said it wasn't. He led us to the boat dock and told me we had to go across the channel. That was when I learned that Marines still held Wilkes Island.

Chapter Thirteen

The Saga of Wilkes

I SUPPOSE "SAGA" MAY SEEM too big a word for the fight of Captain Platt's small detachment of Marines on Wilkes Island, but I have thought about it for four years and I cannot think of a better word for what they did.

Captain Platt, a casual South Carolinian, had sixty Marines to defend Wilkes—sixty men to defend an island one mile long and one-eight of a mile in width. His 5-inch battery, commanded by Lieutenant McAlister, was emplaced near Kuku Point. His 3-inch guns, commanded by Gunner McKinstry, lacked any fire control equipment and were set up for beach defense about midway along the shore. Along the beach between the 3-inch position and Kuku Point there were four .50 caliber machine gun emplacements, while .30 caliber machine guns were spotted on the lagoon side of the island and also to cover the seaward entrance of the small boat channel. Captain Platt had six men at his CP near the middle of the island, not far from the searchlight position.

When the first false report of a landing on Peale Island came over the air raid warning network, Captain Platt ordered Lieutenant McAlister to send one section of 5-inch men to reinforce the machine guns defending the lagoon side while the rest of the battery deployed as infantry along the seaward beach.

They waited. It was too dark to see the man next to you, and rain squalls whipped across the island. At 1:20 a.m., Gunner McKinstry telephoned from the 3-inch positon:

"Captain, I think I hear a motor turning over."

Could he see anything?

"Not a damn thing, but I'm sure it's there. I can hear it."

The sound was faint, muffled by the sea and the intermittent rain. There was a chance that tracer bullets might give light enough to reveal whatever it was in the darkness just offshore. So Captain Platt ordered the .50's to fire at the sound. Those were the first shots of the last day's battle. It was about the time that the Jap destroyers were sighted racing in toward the reef on Wake proper.

The streaking light of the tracer fire showed McAlister a big landing boat close to the beach. It was coming in. He called Platoon Sergeant Bedell, bull-voiced Bedell.

"Send two men to grenade that boat."

Bedell said, "Yes, sir."

But instead of sending two men to the beach, down there in the darkness, to try to smash the Jap landing before they got ashore, Bedell told Pfc William Buehler, "Come along." With all the grenades they could carry, they ran toward the beach, stumbling in the sand, trying to get into water close enough to the landing boat to toss in their grenades, but the boat was already grating in the shallows. Bedell hurled a grenade. It fell short. The Japs were coming ashore, blasting the darkness with fire. Bedell and Buehler could not get close enough to throw their grenades into the boat, but they kept trying. They stood in the path of the Jap's advance, throwing their grenades at the crowded beach the Japs were trying to cross until Bedell fell and Buehler, wounded, was out of grenades. Then Pfc Buehler

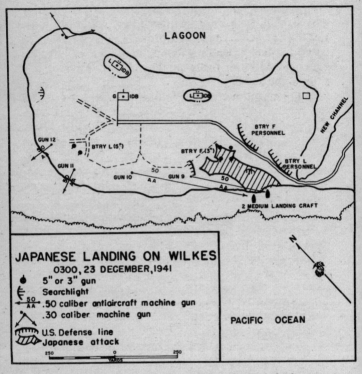

JAPANESE LANDING ON WILKES
0300, 23 DECEMBER, 1941

5" or 3" gun
Searchlight
.50 caliber antiaircraft machine gun
.30 caliber machine gun
U.S. Defense line
Japanese attack

LAGOON

BTRY F PERSONNEL

BTRY L PERSONNEL

NEW CHANNEL

GUN 12

BTRY L (5")

BTRY F (3")

GUN 11

GUN 10

GUN 9

2 MEDIUM LANDING CRAFT

PACIFIC OCEAN

stumbled back through the bullet-splashed darkness to McAlister.

"Sir, they got Bedell. He's dead."

Pfc Buehler did not bother to mention that he was wounded. He took his place in the line. The Japs were coming in from the beach with bayonets. The .50's were raising hell, the tracers spearing fire through the windy darkness, but for each man in that line the battle was only what happened on the ground where he stood. He could not see what was to the left or to the right or even in front of him until a yelling shape came lunging out of the dark, close enough almost to touch. One Marine saw a dim figure spring out of the darkness.

He lunged with his bayonet. They both fell, the Marine and the Jap, each with the other's bayonet in his body. But the line held. The charge broke. For those men, the battle became a deadly game of blindman's bluff, the Japs and Marines firing at the flash of each other's rifles in the night.

In the meantime, while Pfc Buehler was throwing his last grenade, Captain Platt telephoned me for permission to illuminate. Permission granted. The searchlight went on, making the beach like day, and the Marines saw that the landing boat was ashore in front of the 3-inch gun position. The Japs were pouring ashore, deploying, moving with fixed bayonets. The light lasted hardly a minute. Then blackness again. Technical Sergeant E.F. Hassig reported to Platt that the light was dead. It had never functioned properly after being blown over in the earlier bombings.

That was when communications failed between my CP and Wilkes Island. From that time on, I did not know what was happening on Wilkes and Captain Platt did not know what was happening anywhere else. His communications were cut not only with Wake proper but with McAlister and McKinstry. The only line he still had was to the .50 caliber machine guns, and now Pfc S.K. Ray was reporting:

"Captain, they're all around me."

Could he keep the gun in action?

"We can try, sir."

There was a wild burst of firing. The Japs were rushing Ray's gun. Then silence. Pfc Ray picked up the phone he had dropped and reported, "We're still here, sir."

Platt called Sergeant Raymond Coulson and told him the .50's had to be kept firing as long as possible. An enlisted man later described Sergeant Coulson as "regulation as hell, hot-tempered as hell and always trying to get extra chow for his men." Now Sergeant Coulson moved out in the darkness with two or three men to try to keep the Japs from closing in on his guns. It was nasty work in the dark, but he kept the guns firing, hitting blindly at the flank of the main Japanese attack. That attack was driving straight inland from the beach to take McKinstry's 3-inch gun position.

The searchlight had lasted long enough for Gunner McKinstry to see that the main attack was being laid right in his lap. He didn't have riflemen enough to stop the Japs. The enemy was so close that the 3-inch gun could not be depressed low enough for direct hits on the boat or the beach. So McKinstry cut his fuses so short that the shots were almost muzzle blast. That fire smashed the enemy's frontal attack, but the Japs kept up heavy fire into the position as they crawled closer and closer in the shrouding darkness, as snipers crawled inland far enough to fire into McKinstry's flanks. Now they were close enough to lob grenades into the position. They were closing in, almost surrounding him, and all McKinstry's men could see of the enveloping enemy were the flashes when they fired. So McKinstry ordered his gunners to remove the firing locks from the guns. Then they fell back in the darkness to infantry position deeper inland.

The Japs moved into the 3-inch positon. They tried to press farther into the island, but McKinstry's riflemen knocked them back. There, too, the battle became a blindfolded duel.

At 4:30 a.m., lacking communication with McAlister and McKinstry, Captain Platt started on a personal reconnaissance, slipping through the darkness to find his men; to try to prepare for the redoubled attack he knew would come with daylight.

On the lagoon side, there had been no fighting. Now in the early dimness, a Pfc saw a Japanese officer walking along the shore. Apparently he had pushed ahead of his men to the lagoon on a checkup. The Pfc watched him a while and then inquired:

"Say, Sergeant, there's a Jap officer down there.

Shall I shoot him?"

Platoon Sergeant Joe Stowe exploded, "Hell, yes, you damn fool, or give me that rifle and I'll do it!"

The Pfc did it.

In that early light, Jap flags were seen in a line directly across Wilkes Island. Those were the flags reported to me. They apparently had been set up by the Japs so that the dive bombers which attacked us as soon as it was light enough would not bomb their own troops.

The bulk of the Japanese were massed in the 3-inch position, which gave them good cover, while their flanks were covered by riflemen and machine guns concealed behind scattered piles of coral. They still heavily outnumbered the Marines, but Captain Platt decided to take them before they started taking him.

Lieutenant McAlister combined forces with Gunner McKinstry—a total of perhaps twenty-five Marines—and began a frontal attack on the Japanese position. Their advance was checked by Japanese firing from behind a big rock. Their fire could not dislodge the Japs, and Gunner McKinstry started forward to scale the rock, but McAlister stopped him.

"'Detail a man for that job," he said.

Before McKinstry could reply, Corporal William C. Halstead started forward. He said, "I got it, Gunner."

McAlister's men kept up a brisk fire at the side of the rock to keep the enemy pinned down while Corporal Halstead went forward. The corporal climbed the rock, pitched grenades down on the Japs and finished them off with his rifle. Then he waved to the others to come on. They moved forward beyond the rock against a slashing fire. That was where Corporal Halstead was killed, going forward.

Meanwhile, Captain Platt had rounded up the crews of two .30 caliber machine guns and eight riflemen. He led them to a position in the rear of the enemy position and there divided his little force, sending Corporal John S. Johnson, Jr., with one gun to the left while he took

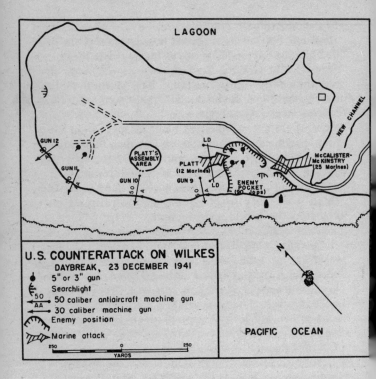

U.S. COUNTERATTACK ON WILKES
DAYBREAK, 23 DECEMBER 1941

● 5" or 3" gun
Searchlight
50 caliber antiaircraft machine gun
30 caliber machine gun
Enemy position
Marine attack

250   0   250
YARDS

the other gun to the right.

The sound of firing told him that McAlister and McKinstry were assaulting the enemy's front. Because of the short distance to those Marines, Platt ordered his men to fire only at targets identified as enemy.

"Fire short bursts," he ordered, "and keep moving."

They hit the Japs from two directions in the rear, firing at ranges of less than fifty yards, blasting their way in to meet the Marines attacking from the front.

In front of the Japs, McAlister swung part of the men to hit the enemy's flank while McKinstry kept going forward with the rest. From the cover of rocks, the

Japs maintained a scathing fire, but the Marines kept advancing. A few Japs played possum among the dead and tried to bayonet Marines as they passed. McKinstry ordered, "Be sure the dead ones are dead." After that, the possum players got nobody. The Marines kept advancing with the bayonet until they met in the Japanese position and swept it clean.

Captain Platt reorganized his force and swept the island, but the enemy's resistance was over. The Japs on Wilkes had been exterminated by a force half their number. The Japs had put one hundred or more men on Wilkes, and the only live Japs on the island when Platt finished mopping up were a couple of hog-tied prisoners and one Jap who was playing dead.

It was 7:40 a.m. The dive bombers hit them, blasting and strafing while the helpless Marines hugged the deck.

At 8 a.m., ships were seen moving in southwest of Wilkes and Captain Platt ordered McAlister to reorganize his battery as artillery and to fire at the ships if they came within range.

Platt's men tore down the Japanese flags, but our observers did not report this to me. Captain Platt still did not know what was happening on Wake or Peale. Over the air raid warning network, he managed to get in touch with the garage at Camp One, but all they could tell him was that there was fighting toward the airfield; that there had been no communication with my CP since soon after the battle began.

About noon, still under dive bombing attack, Platt's watchers reported a destroyer had moved in only two thousand yards from the channel entrance and that several other ships were within four thousand yards off shore. Platt ordered McAlister's 5-inch guns to engage the enemy, but McAlister reported that both guns had been knocked out by bombs. They could not be repaired.

Watchers reported a considerable number of small boats moving in toward Wake near the channel. Lacking artillery to fire on them, Captain Platt gathered all the men he could and ordered an advance to the channel as infantry to repel the boats. As they trudged wearily through the coral and brush, the dive bombers attacked them again. Pfc Robert L. Stevens was killed. He was the last Marine casualty of the battle of Wake Island.

Meanwhile, as Platt's dog-tired men slogged toward the channel, we were crossing to Wilkes Island in a launch. The sword-swinging jg had about thirty Japs to guard us, but he made sure that Sergeant Malleck and I were up forward with our white flag. When we landed on Wilkes, I shouted:

"This is Major Devereux! The island has been surrendered! Put down your arms!"

Nobody answered. We walked slowly along the beach, Malleck and I in the lead with our white flag. The Japs fingered their rifles nervously as they followed.

I shouted, "The island has been surrendered! Don't try any monkey business!"

There was no answer. We heard nobody; saw nobody. The only sign of life was the Jap shipping offshore. Destroyers as well as landing craft from the big ships were closing in. Though I did not know it, those were the boats that Platt's men were coming to repel with rifles and machine guns.

I saw a flash from one of the destroyers. A shell burst at the water's edge. A moment later, a second shell exploded. It was nearer. We were the target. Sergeant Malleck and I kept walking straight ahead. We knew we ought to hit the deck, but without saying a word we were both damned if we would duck while the sword-swinging jg was on his feet.

We kept walking. The third shell burst within fifty yards of us. I wanted to crawl into a hole. I am sure Sergeant Malleck must have wished the same thing. But we kept walking. We were scared, but we could not show it before the Japs.

Then the Jap jg did what he should have done at the first shot. He told all hands to take shelter and ordered a signalman to give the destroyer the word to cease fire. I have never been more relieved than when that Jap officer took cover so I could, too.

After the signalman had stopped the destroyer's fire, we went on. I kept calling out from time to time that the island had surrendered, but we were halfway to Ku-ku Point before I saw any troops—a few grubby, dirty men who came out of the brush with their rifles ready, sullen-eyed, unwilling to believe even when they heard me call that we had surrendered. A moment later, Captain Platt appeared with his officers.

I told them, "We have surrendered."

Platt was looking at me. His mouth was a tight line. He said, "Yes, sir."

The irrepressible Platt was soon kidding with our captors as we moved on to the 3-inch gun position where so many of the Japanese had been slaughtered. When we reached the position, the Japs started jabbering as they stared at the litter of dead. Hearing them one of the corpses stood up. He was wounded, not seriously, and he had been playing dead. He fawned over us, but he was different when I saw him later on a stretcher. Somebody had given me a canteen and I offered him a drink of water, but he pushed the canteen aside contemptuously. He was among hundreds of his own people then, and by this time he knew we were helpless, so he wanted to show how tough he was.

At Platt's CP, the Japs released the two prisoners. One of them burst into tears and ran to a dead Jap sprawled on the coral. He kept sobbing and saying "My brother . . . my brother . . . "

Several hundred Japs under a full lieutenant landed on Wilkes from the boats Platt had been going to meet. Our sword-swinging jg giggled a lot as he made his report, apparently feeling pretty good that we had not run into trouble, but his superior was not amused. The lieutenant kept scowling at us. I imagine he had learned how many men that day's work had cost them.

One of the officers ordered Gunner McKinstry to get into a truck. McKinstry asked me, "What are they going to do? Shoot me?"

I said, "Nonsense. You've got nothing to worry about."

He had not had a minute's sleep for twenty-four hours. Now the Japs started him to work, driving him for another twenty-four hours, and whenever he dozed off they woke him up with a bayonet.

When we reached the channel where the prisoners were being gathered for transportation to Wake proper, I saw one of Platt's men who was desperately wounded. Platt asked the Jap officer to let him be taken to Wake for medical attention at once, but the Jap pretended not to understand and kept the wounded Marine there until all the prisoners were gathered. When at last we did cross the channel, Platt found some officers who spoke a little English and urged them to let us send the badly wounded man ahead to the hospital. They only shrugged.

They made plain they were not concerned about our wounded. They had wounded of their own to care for.

Platt spied a Jap with a big black sword strapped to his back and exclaimed, "Whew, Major, look at that! I wonder what it's for?" I guessed it was an executioner's sword, but Platt asked the Jap, "What's that for?" The Jap just grinned.

We saw the Jap landing force commander, the Navy captain with the wounded hand, talking to Commander Cunningham and Commander Keene. When they got in a truck with some other American officers, Platt, McAlister and I climbed in after them. Nobody tried to stop us. We drove to the Jap headquarters near Hanna's gun, where the Jap commander continued to question Cunningham and Keene. Commander Keene was drawing diagrams to show Wake's facilities for food, water, shelter and so on, when the Jap commander interrupted him by taking the pad and pencil to write one question:

"Where are women's quarters?"

Keene wrote: "No women on island."

The Jap commander looked at him as though Keene had announced that black was white.

The Jap officers offered us some canned food. It was now about 2:00 p.m. and I had not eaten since six o'clock the night before, so even that raw fish tasted good. But as I ate it, I felt dead inside. Maybe it was partly exhaustion. I had just walked six miles under guard, most of the time with my hands in the air, and my body ached from weariness and from lack of sleep, but I do not think that was the reason I felt as I did. I think it was simply that at last the full realization came of what had happened. We had done our best and it had not been good enough. It was what I have called "the death of pride." I suppose you could call it despair.

They were marching prisoners toward us now. Most of the men were stripped to their skivvies. Some had lost even their shoes and were limping barefooted on the coral. They were exhausted, hungry, dirty and there was no hope. They had been shambling along, trailing after Sergeant Hassig, a barrel-chested man whose pride in life was his stripes and his bushy moustache. It was a regular Guards moustache and it bristled as he told the straggling men:

"Snap outta this stuff! God damn it, you're Marines!"

A few moments later, they passed where we were eating our raw fish. Sergeant Hassig was at right guide, shoulders back, moustache defiant. And the men—weary scarecrows—were marching in perfect cadence, heads up and eyes front, stepping out like a regiment on parade. The Jap guards had to trot to keep up with them.

I felt pride at the sight of them marching by, at the

bewilderment on the faces of the Japanese officers standing with me. The Japanese never did understand. As they used to say, "But you don't act like prisoners!"

Captain Koyama of the Imperial Japanese Navy, in an interrogation after the war, said of the fight for Wilkes, "In general, that part of the operation was not successful." I believe everyone will agree that this was a masterpiece of understatement.

U.S. Marine Corps Photos

During formal ceremonies that brought Wake under U.S. military control again, Brig. Gen. Lawson H.M. Sanderson, USMC, and his party stand at attention; second from left, at his rear, stands Col. Walter J. Bayler, "the last man off Wake Island." *Below*, a platoon of Japanese army and navy officers, headed by Rear Admiral Shigematsu Sakaibara (extreme left), stand at attention during the reading of the proclamation.

Alex L. Martin

Major James P.S. Devereux receives the sword of the former prison camp commander of the Hakodate Branch PW Camp No. 3, Hokkaido, Japan, on September 11, 1945.

Alex L. Martin

Wake Island veterans line up at their PW camp on Hokkaido after being liberated. Major Devereux is at right in officer group.

Almost four years after departure, Major Devereux arrives at Pearl Harbor on September 9, 1945.

(Left) After better than four years, Major Devereux and his son Paddy are reunited. *(Bottom)* Major Devereux, accompanied by Paddy, is accorded a rousing "welcome home" by the residents of Chevy Chase, Maryland.

(*Above*) Now a colonel, James Devereux is back to duty on January 26 1946, at the Marine Barracks, Quantico, Virginia. *Below*, President Dwight Eisenhower signs a bill authored by Congressman Devereux, re turning the frigate *U.S.S. Constellation* to permanent mooring in Balti more. Originally built in Baltimore in 1797, the *Constellation* was the firs naval vessel to capture a foreign warship; it was declared a historica landmark in 1964.

Defenders of Wake Island gather for 1978 reunion at Oklahoma City. *(Top, from left)* Pvt. Ed Eaton of Kansas City, Kansas; Pvt. Rudy Slezak of Pueblo, Colorado; Seaman 1st Class Floyd Dixon of Houston, Texas; and Pfc Armand Benjamin of San Diego, Calif. *(Bottom, from left)* Pvt. Edward Sturgeon of Richview, Illinois; Pfc George Stringfield of Norman, Oklahoma; and Pfc Robby Robinson. Military ranks are from 1941.

Wake Islanders at 1978 reunion (1941 military ranks): *(top)* Sgt. Raymo~~n~~ Gragg of Beaverton, Oregon; *(middle left)* Major James Devereux; *(middle right)* Sgt. Bernard Manning of Winter Park, Florida; *(lower left)* Pvt. Tony Oubre of Fallbrook, California; and Lt. Bob Hanna of Lak~~e~~ Como, Florida.

Chapter Fourteen

" . . . And a Happy New Year"

IT WAS AN EXPENSIVE VICTORY for the Japanese. First figures made available to us indicated Wake Island cost them 11 naval ships, 29 planes and more than 5,700 men killed. The American losses were a dozen planes and 96 dead. Our dead included 46 Marines, 47 civilians and three sailors. In the final attack on December 23, the Japs admitted the loss of one destroyer and 350 dead in addition to the two destroyers which they beached and which were gutted by Lieutenant Hanna's fire. The American loss in the final attack was 26 dead, including a dozen civilians.

The matter of total enemy losses in men and equipment is subject to very considerable uncertainty. In fact, no accurate records exist to verify anyone's estimates. I believe the early figures given by the Japanese are exaggerated, probably because of their proclivity for saying what they know the listener wants to hear.

Later, according to estimates published in a Navy monograph after the war, which were compiled from studies of captured documents and POW interrogations, the Japanese losses were approximately 820 killed and 333 wounded for a total of 1,153. They say that the enemy lost at least four warships sunk and that a minimum of eight ships sustained appreciable damage.

Twenty-one aircraft were shot down by fighters or anti-aircraft and eleven more left the atoll in damaged condition. They then say, somewhat confusingly, that a total of *51* aircraft sustained reportable damage from Wake's antiaircraft batteries.

No one will ever know the accurate numbers, but all can agree that we made the Japs pay a full price for the island. In the words of Commander Masatake Okumiya of the Imperial Navy, "Considering the power accumulated for the invasion of Wake Island, and the meager forces of the defenders, it was one of the most humiliating defeats the Japanese Navy had ever suffered."

While the Japs were still rounding us up, even before the order to surrender had reached all hands, it became apparent that the Japanese had a list of all American officers on Wake Island. It was mimeographed in Japanese, but I heard them checking it and the last name on the list—where it would normally have appeared in a similar list of our own—was that of Gunner Hamas.

I learned much later one method Jap agents in Hawaii used to keep track of ship and troop movements. They used Japanese girls who regularly invited service men to picnics and parties. They saw to it that the service men had a good time so they would be eager to come again. Thus when none of the men from a particular ship or unit appeared for a picnic, the Jap agents would know that the ship or that unit had left Hawaii. When members of the ship's crew again appeared for their regular dates, the spies would know the ship had returned. The time the ship had been gone and its type usually enabled them to make a shrewd guess where it had gone and frequently what it had been doing. If the members of land units disappeared at the same time, the spies could guess with a good chance of accuracy where those units had gone. I am not suggesting that this was the method by which the Japanese learned the names of the officers on Wake Island because I have no idea how they did pull the trick. All I know is that despite the fact we all came to Wake under secret orders and at several different times, the Japanese apparently did have a list of officers on the island.

The Japanese were especially interested in Captain Wilson, the Army officer in charge of the radio trailer. They had him listed for special attention for something that had happened in 1939 when a Japanese naval training vessel was docked in Hawaii. Captain Wilson, then a civilian customs inspector, attempted to board the Jap vessel, but was halted on the dock by an arrogant sentry. The sentry insisted that Wilson bow low and salute the Japanese flag. Wilson drew his pistol and drove the sentry ahead of him as he boarded the ship without a bow or a salute. The Japanese consul apologized profusely for the incident, but the Japs didn't forget Wilson. And after the surrender on Wake two years later, they called him to account for the insult. A Jap officer informed him:

"You are responsible for the war between Nippon and the United States. You stirred up animosity. For that you will be decapitated."

Captain Wilson started talking for his life. He insisted that the Wilson they wanted was another Wilson, explaining that Wilson was a very common name among Americans, like Smith or Jones or Brown. His clinching argument was:

"The Wilson in Hawaii was a civilian customs inspector. But I am an Army officer."

The Japanese admitted there was no doubt that the Wilson they wanted was a civilian customs inspector. Nor was there any doubt that the prisoner Wilson was an Army officer. The only logical conclusion was that the two could not be the same person, even though they had the same initials, and so the Japs let Captain Wilson live. The Japanese have very few family names, so the coincidence seemed quite understandable to them.

By sunset that day, December 23, all Americans on

Wake had been rounded up. Thirty-seven years later, Corporal Franklin D. Gross vividly recalls the way it was for him and his men.

"When it began to get light that morning, we saw dozens of ships. We heard later that the Japanese believed Wake Island was strongly defended. Then I got word by phone to bring my men to the command post.

"On the way, we were captured by a squad of Japanese soldiers. They huddled us into a group and tied wire around our necks, down our backs and around our wrists. Then they set up a machine gun six feet away.

"Now, all through the 1930s we believed all the propaganda that Marines didn't surrender. We had never been told any differently. We hadn't been issued dog tags or told our serial numbers. We just knew they were going to shoot us then and there, and we were calm . . . we had accepted our fate.

"I was surprised when, instead, they shoved us into a small room in the hospital. There were several hundred men in that room. Some were dying and some were wounded.

"After several hours they took us to the airfield, which was graveled, and not concrete as later ones were. Here we lay for 2½ days in just our underwear. It got cold at night, and we had a half piece of bread a day. We drank water from cans that had held gasoline, and the stench was so strong you could set your breath on fire after taking a drink. The truth was, the Japanese were not equipped to handle prisoners."

By nightfall, ten of us had been separated from the rest of the men and confined in the one-room cottage we called the White House. Sergeant Malleck was the only enlisted man among us.

Ten men crowded the single room, but we were too exhausted to care. We were sprawled out, each man thinking his own bitter thoughts, too tired to talk, when our guard snapped to attention at the door. A Japanese admiral walked in, resplendent in stiffly starched whites with a lot of decorations and a sword. We were told he was the commander of the task force which had taken the island. He looked at us sternly as we stood up. Then he handed a paper to Commander Cunningham who read it aloud. We kept a copy of it:

PROCLAMATION

Here it is proclaimed that the entire islands of Wake are now the state-property of the Great Empire of Japan.

PUBLIC NOTICE

The Great Empire of Japan who loves peace and respects justice has been obliged to take arms against the challenge of President Roosevelt. Therefore, in accordance with the peace-loving spirit of the Great Empire of Japan, Japanese Imperial Navy will not inflict any harms on those people—though they have been our enemy—who do not hold hostility against us in any respect. So, they be in peace!

But whoever violates our spirit or whoever are not obedient shall be severely punished by our martial law.

issued by
THE HEADQUARTERS OF JAPANESE IMPERIAL NAVY

We noticed two curious things about the admiral's proclamation. First, in both places where the word "Navy" appeared, it had been written on a tiny bit of paper and carefully pasted over some other word, presumably "Army." Second, the phrase "those people" obviously referred to a native population, though Wake had none and the Japs must have known that as well as we did. It was just an attempt to blow up their victory to a bigger size for propaganda at home, as they did, in fact, in newspaper articles which referred to Camp One and Camp Two as "cities" captured by the valorous Japanese Navy in the conquest of Wake.

When Commander Cunningham finished reading the proclamation, we sat down and lit cigarettes. Somebody offered the Jap admiral a cigarette, but he angrily waved it aside. He stood glaring at us, outraged at our lack of reaction to the proclamation and doubtless at our failure to stand submissively awaiting his pleasure. He took his peeve out on the sentry with an explosive harangue in Japanese, and every time he had to pause for breath, the sentry gave him a bow and yelped, *"Hai!"* We gathered that meant, "Aye, aye, sir!" The admiral finally got tired of talking and stalked out, and the sentry relaxed at the door.

Even then, as we fell asleep under the sentry's eye, I think most of us expected to be rescued. We knew that ships were due next day to evacuate the civilians and we still assumed they would be part of a task force bringing us reinforcements, but the next day the only ships we saw were the vessels of the Japanese force around the island. Our Christmas dinner at the White House consisted of crackers and evaporated milk.

A long time later I learned that we were right in assuming that an American task force had been on its way to Wake. The task force, built around the aircraft carrier *Saratoga,* was only twenty-four hours from Wake when we surrendered. The force was ordered to turn back. The Navy had too little left after Pearl Harbor to gamble the ships on an attempt to retake Wake. They wrote us off. I have been told that when they saw the task force was turning back without striking a blow at the Jap force around Wake Island, pilots on the *Saratoga* sat down on the flight deck and cried.

The ten of us in the White House were not allowed to communicate with the other prisoners, but we were fed fairly well and were not abused, so we assumed that the other prisoners were being similarly treated. We did not learn how wrong we were until a note was smuggled in to us by a prisoner bringing our food the day after Christmas. Then we learned of the reasonless brutality to which our comrades were being subjected.

I have mentioned how prisoners were partly stripped as they surrendered, many being stripped down to their underwear, and how their hands were bound behind them with telephone wire. Their tightly bound hands were pulled high up their backs so that the muscles ached and then one end of the wire was noosed around their necks so they would choke themselves if they tried to free their hands or even tried to lessen the tortuous strain. Some were left bound even after every American on the island had been rounded up and all were safely under guard.

Even sick and wounded, even some still bleeding, were trussed like the others and herded along as the Japanese packed scores of prisoners into the hospital dugouts, prodding them with bayonets, pushing them into space already so crowded there was hardly room for men to stand. Gunner Hamas was one of them and he says the place was "packed to the point of suffocation." Men fainted from lack of air, but the others could not help them; could not free bound hands to loosen the nooses that threatened to strangle the unconscious men. Men were vomiting on each other. There was no air; only stench.

Gunner Hamas had picked up a little Japanese while doing duty in Shanghai and he risked a bayonet to call to an elderly Jap officer strolling past the entrance. He asked the officer to free Dr. Kahn so he could attend the wounded and a man who was dying.

The Jap replied in English, "You doctor, too?"

"No, sir."

"Are you an officer?"

"Yes, sir."

The officer ordered sentries to free the doctor and Gunner Hamas. He gave them a few cigarettes and matches. The doctor tried to aid the wounded and the sick, but there was little they could do in the crowded dugout except save the unconscious men from choking themselves to death.

The elderly Jap officer came back a little later and Hamas tackled him again. He showed him how badly the hands of the men were swollen from the pressure of the tight wire, and the Jap allowed him to loosen the wire around the prisoners' necks and hands. A little later, the Jap allowed them to take off the wire and allowed some of the prisoners to leave the fetid dugout and sleep in the open, under guard. He also let Hamas gather up some clothing discarded in the road for the prisoners, though this angered a sentry so he jabbed Hamas in the hip with his bayonet.

Then the prisoners were moved to the airstrip. Most of those who left the stinking dugout had their underwear or little more. They dug with their bare hands into the hardpacked coral to make shallow holes so they would have some protection against the chilling wind.

They had to work the next day, but they received no food. The Japs cooked a meal for them and then deliberately let it spoil. The first water they got was brought in gasoline drums. The water was so tainted with gasoline that men retched as they forced themselves to drink.

When the note telling of the treatment of the prisoners was smuggled to us at the White House, I wrote a letter to the commander of the Jap landing force requesting that he give the other officers and men food, clothing and shelter. I showed the letter to Commander Keene because Commander Cunningham had been moved from the White House, leaving Commander Keene senior officer present. It met with his approval. The Jap commander did not answer my letter, but we learned soon afterward that the men had been moved into barracks and that they were being fed.

Dr. Kahn and Dr. Shark were allowed to move our sick and wounded to a building, but they had almost nothing with which to treat their patients. The Japs had taken almost all of our medical supplies and showed no interest in whether the American patients lived or died. Not that their own wounded were very much better off. The Japanese had been praised for the efficiency of their sanitary corps during the Russo-Japanese War, but on Wake the Japanese medical men seemed to have no interest in even the rudiments of sanitation. Dr. Kahn told me that the Jap never destroyed a bloody bandage; they simply threw it out the window. As a result, the hospital was heavy with stench and swarmed with flies.

Our men were not subjected to brutality after my protest, but there was the constant threat of execution over our heads. Typical was the time the Japs ordered Dan Teters to supervise the removal of dynamite we had buried under the airstrip. Teters tried to explain that he had not buried it and so he could not be sure he would find all the dynamite pockets. The Jap officer wouldn't listen to excuses.

"You'd better find them all," the Jap said. "Don't forget we can stand you out there when we try the exploder."

Captain Tharin, Gunner Hamas and about thirty Marines were assigned the task of gathering our dead and burying them. Some of the dead had been placed in the reefer, but the refrigeration machinery had been knocked out by bombs and the bodies were badly decomposed. The men ordered to get those bodies were so hungry that in the stench-filled reefer they greedily ate the only food they found there, several big jars of maraschino cherries. Four years later, safe in the States, the taste of a maraschino cherry was enough to make Corporal Brown vomit.

The dead were buried in a single grave near Hanna's gun. The men dug the grave four feet deep and laid the dead side by side in the trench. They covered the bodies with rubber ponchos, weighting down the ponchos with heavy chunks of coral, and then they filled the trench and made a long, low mound. The burial service was simple. The men who dug the grave stood bareheaded while somebody said a prayer and then the guards took them back.

The Japs were calling some of us from the White House for questioning every day. My first interrogation was by a smart aleck whose need of a haircut told me that his commission was brand new, but he thought he was a bearcat at shrewd questioning.

He asked, "How did you know the war had begun?"

"We got a message from Pearl Harbor."

"How did you know we were going to attack Wake?"

"We didn't know."

"Didn't you know our planes were coming?"

"No."

"Well, how did you know they were coming?"

"We didn't know until they arrived."

"Didn't you have any detection apparatus? You know what I mean."

I knew he was hinting at radar, and I answered, "No, we had none at all."

Then he screwed up his face ferociously and demanded, "you must draw me a picture of such things!"

I couldn't help laughing. I said, "Me? I don't know anything about them."

A child should have known it without asking, but I had to explain at length that such instruments required specially trained men to operate them and that nobody who was not a specialist could give him a scientific description. He was finally convinced and sent me back to the White House.

My interrogation by the task force commander's chief of staff struck me as almost equally silly. Wake Island had been Japanese for two weeks when he called me out to his car and asked me to show him where my guns were emplaced. I was not telling him anything he did not know already, so I pointed out the positions, but it took some time to convince the chief of staff I wasn't holding out on him. After I heard the questions he had asked other officers, it seemed obvious to me that even the Japanese top command could not understand the efficiency of our 5-inch batteries and they were still worried by the suspicion that we must have larger guns hidden somewhere.

All this time, despite guards and chain gang discipline and the danger of execution, the enlisted Marines were still carrying on the war by sabotage. The Japs gathered up all our weapons and put prisoners to work cleaning them, preparing the weapons for use by the Japanese. The Marines submissively cleaned the rifles, polishing the outside of each rifle until it shone brightly enough for a presidential inspection—and then poured salt water down the barrels so the rifles would soon be useless.

We had destroyed our fire control equipment, but some of the 3-inch guns were still serviceable and the Japs were jubilant at these additions to the anti-aircraft defense they were installing. The Marines assigned to clean these guns made them bright and shiny—and slipped sand into the recoil mechanism.

Marines detailed to clean the captured machine guns managed to palm small, vital parts such as sears and later threw them far into the brush. The guns looked beautiful, but they would not be much use in a battle.

The Japs found a supply of primers for the 5-inch guns which had not been destroyed, and a Marine obligingly showed them how to use the primers. The Marine fired a primer, and the Jap nodded sagely at the *Pop!* So the Marine fired another and kept demonstrating how to use the primers until none was left.

It makes a good tale now and we can smile at the way the Japs were fooled, but it was not amusing then. Each of those Marines gambled his life every time he palmed a sear or poured salt water down a rifle barrel. If he was caught or even suspected, he would have become a job for the Japanese executioner we saw now and then stalking about with his big sword strapped to his back. Yet on the captured island and afterward during the years our men were slaving in mines and on work projects in prison camps, their sabotage continued. They seemed always willing to risk their necks to get in another lick at the enemy.

In the White House, we learned little of this until much later. When we were not being interrogated, we were allowed to read, play cards, take short strolls under guard and wash our clothes. We tried to persuade the Jap interpreter to let us rescue our toothbrushes from our gear, but he refused.

"There are many people in Japan who have no toothbrushes," he said.

He bragged that he was a graduate of Columbia University, and maybe he was, but we called him "Garters" because he wore socks and exposed Paris-style garters with his shorts. Whenever one of us was called for questioning, Garters was in his glory. He would escort the prisoner to headquarters, swaggering along with a ferocious air, brandishing his pistol as though only he and his pistol prevented a general jailbreak.

At night when the island was blacked out, we tried to amuse ourselves by playing guessing games like "Who Am I?" or by talking with our succession of guards. They were all tough, husky men and most of them were amiable and dumb as well. Almost every one of them would point at his nose as an American might tap his chest and proclaim himself the Judo champion of Japan by declaring, "Me Number One Judo." They all were eager to exhibit their skill, but we refused because we knew we would lose face if we were thrown or even if we had bodily contact.

They were proud of the little English they had picked up even though frequently they had no idea of the meaning of the phrases they parroted. One of the them was always eager to recite, over and over, as long as we would listen:

> God save our gracious king,
> Long live our noble king,
> God save the king!

We always told him his pronunciation was good and he always beamed like a small boy receiving an unexpected ice cream cone. He had a rival who couldn't recite, but who made his bid for approval one night by giving a demonstration of Japanese scouting and patrolling, what we call "sneaking and peeking." The Jap stalked imaginary enemies around the room until Captain Platt said, "Here let me show you how the Americans do it." Platt held out his hand for the rifle—and the Jap gave it to him!

Our life in the White House was tedious and galling, but all of us were to look back on it as a time of comparative contentment and even luxury. We got an inkling of what was ahead, on January 11, 1942, when they told us we were being shipped out next day on a prison ship. They posted this notice:

> *Commander of the Prisoner Escort*
> *Navy of the Great Japanese Empire*

REGULATIONS FOR PRISONERS

The prisoners disobeying the following orders will be punished with immediate death:

(a) Those disobeying orders and instructions.

(b) Those showing a motion of antagonism and raising a sign of opposition.

(c) Those disordering the regulations by individualism, egoism, thinking only about yourself, rushing for your own goods.

(d) Those talking without permission and raising loud voices.

(e) Those walking and moving without order.

(f)   Those carrying unnecessary baggage in embark-
      ing.

(g)   Those resisting mutually.

(h)   Those touching the boat's materials, wires, elec-
      tric lights, tools, switches, etc.

(i)   Those climbing ladder without order.

(j)   Those showing action of running away from the
      room or boat.

(k)   Those trying to take more meal than given to
      them.

(l)   Those using more than two blankets.

These twelve capital crimes were followed by five
paragraphs of detailed intructions, ending on this
hopeful note:

> Navy of the Great Japanese Empire will not try
> to punish you all with death. Those obeying all
> rules and regulations, and believing the action and
> purpose of the Japanese Navy, co-operating with
> Japan in constructing the "New Order of the Great
> Asia" which leads to the world's peace will be well
> treated.

Since immediate death was the punishment for taking
"unnecessary baggage" aboard the prison ship, we
asked Garters how much baggage was considered necessary.

"I don't know," Garters said.

"Well, does it mean one bag or two?"

"I don't know," he said.

"Will you find out?"

"No, I can't find out."

Garters showed no more interest in the discussion.
After all, it wasn't his neck. To be on the safe side,
we decided that each of us would take only one bag.
In mine I packed some underwear, socks and handker-
chiefs, a raincoat, a pack of cards, a pair of shoes

that didn't fit me, a toothbrush I had found and scalded, and an envelope containing personal papers. The landing force commander had examined the papers, which concerned only my family, and had put his "chop" on them authorizing me to take them. In addition to my bag, I had only the clothes I wore: khaki slacks and shirt, tennis shoes, a leather windbreaker, a battered sun helmet and a handkerchief in my pocket. We were forbidden to take even cigarettes.

On the morning of January 12, the Japs began loading enlisted men and civilians aboard the *Nitta Maru,* a liner which had been converted into a prison ship. About three quarters of the civilians were being shipped with us, while the rest were remaining on Wake with all the seriously wounded. Dr. Shark, the civilian doctor, whose courage and devotion to duty were outstanding through the battle, was one of the civilians left on Wake. I have never since been able to find any trace of him and I fear he may have been executed on the island.

Most of the Americans we left on Wake were subsequently shipped to Japanese prison camps. On the night of October 7, 1943, the Japanese, with the excuse that the ninety-eight American civilians still on the island had established secret radio communication with United States naval forces, lined up the Americans on the beach and murdered them with machine guns. For this crime, the Jap commander on Wake—Rear Admiral Shigematsu Sakaibara—and eleven of his officers were sentenced to hang after trial by an American naval court at Kwajalein following the Japanese capitulation. After my release, in meeting Brigadier General Lawson Sanderson, USMC, who took the surrender of Wake, I learned that it was apparent the Japs on Wake were short of food due to constant patrolling by our submarines. To a Jap, that would be reason enough to massacre prisoners.

Late in the afternoon we were put aboard a landing

craft. There I met Major Potter for the first time since the surrender.

"Well, Jimmy, here we are! Don't look so glum. Things will be all right."

I tried to act cheerful, too, but I didn't feel it. We soon had still less reason to feel optimistic. When we came alongside the *Nitta Maru,* a cargo net was lowered. We threw in our bags and piled on top of them. The Japs hoisted the net and dumped us on the deck where a line of Jap sailors were waiting with clubs. As we scrambled over each to get our bags, we were ordered to go below past the line of sailors. They did not hit us, but I learned that the enlisted men and civilians had been forced to run the gauntlet of clubs.

Corporal Gross was one of those who were beaten. "Everybody made it," he said, "although I wonder how. As we boarded, the Japanese began kicking and hitting us, and then herded us down into the holds, where we were jammed in."

We were stopped at the foot of the ladder while our bags were inspected. I was afraid the inspector would not see the Jap's commander "chop" on my papers and leaned forward to point it out to him. A guard slapped me in the face as hard as he could. Nobody had ever slapped me before, and I was so surprised I could only gasp, which was probably lucky. By the time I recovered, we had been shoved down two more ladders and a Jap was spraying us with disinfectant. We were not stripped, so I don't see that the spraying did anybody any good except the Jap who seemed to enjoy squirting the stuff on us.

We were herded into a steel-walled compartment about thirty feet square. It had been the mail storage room when the ship was in commercial service. There were no portholes; not even a basin. The only furnishings were straw ticks which littered the floor and a raised platform that ran around the bulkhead.

We bathed by wetting a rag with mouthwash and wiping our faces. We were fed twice a day—a meal of weak, tasteless rice gruel or a single small fish, sometimes with two olives or a piece of radish added as a special treat. The lights burned all the time, and a guard with a bayonet stood at the open door to see that we did not whisper among ourselves. Once Captain Platt was accused of whispering and the guard beat him with the stick. None of us tried to interfere. We were of the opinion that if we, as leaders, attempted resistance, the Japs would not only execute us but would murder many of our men. And their hardships were many, sometimes brutal, even with us holding ourselves in check.

Looking back on those days aboard the *Nitta Maru*, Corporal Franklin Gross was to say in 1978:

"I knew I was starving. We had a cup of barley water twice a day with a teaspoon of barley in it. At first, we were in tropical waters and it was unbearably hot in our crowded hold. This was reversed when we got to northern waters—we nearly froze.

"There was a pile of old dirty clothes and we were told to grab something. I got a pair of trousers which had belonged to a man who had been strafed in the legs and they were stiff with dried blood.

"Incidentally, the guy who owned those trousers, Corporal Ralph Holewinski, is now a sheriff in Gaylord, Michigan.

"We didn't know at the time, but we later found out that five of our group were taken up and beheaded as a sports spectacle for the ship's company. The men were selected at random, and it could very easily have been me. These murders came out during the war crimes trials after the war. Incredibly, the Japanese officer responsible for giving the order escaped custody and, to the best of my knowledge, was never recaptured."

After five days of this, the *Nitta Maru* reached Yokohama. Cunningham, Keene, Teters and I were taken to a bitterly cold stateroom where we shivered in our tropic clothing while a Jap—a member of the secret police, we thought—questioned us about the things the Japanese already knew: How many military on Wake? How many civilians?

The next day eight officers and a dozen enlisted men were taken ashore. The officers were Major Putnam, Major Potter, Lieutenant Kliewer and Gunner Borth, of the Marines, and Commander Keene and Ensigns Olcott, Henshaw and Lauff, of the Navy. We never knew why these officers were picked out, but later we guessed it was because they presented a cross-section of the Wake establishment—the defense battalion, VMF 211, the naval air station and naval communications, a further indication of the Japs' special interest in our radio.

There wasn't any time for farewells; nothing beyond, "So long, we'll be seeing you one of these days." We had been ordered to surrender our watches and jewelry before reaching Yokohama, but Major Putnam had left his wrist watch hidden in the overhead. I found it after he was taken ashore. I wore it through our captivity and returned it to Putnam when we met in the States after our release.

We sailed from Yokohama January 19, and the next night the door of our prison was locked for the first time. The word was that a submarine was tracking us. If that submarine had sunk the *Nitta Maru*, it would have been quite unpleasant.

On January 23, the engines stopped. Nobody knew where we were. Then the officers were ordered on deck. I gawked at what I saw—we were tied up at the Bund in Shanghai. I had been there in 1930 and now I was so busy trying to identify landmarks that at first I hardly felt the raw, biting cold.

Japanese and Chinese reporters came aboard, snapped pictures of us and gave us some cigarettes. Then we were herded below again, and next morning in the bitter cold we were marched ashore at Woosung, a few miles below Shanghai. There the Japanese Army took us over from the Navy.

The Japs had put up posters all along our route of march inviting the Chinese to watch the parade of the captives, proof of the invincible valor of Japanese arms, but only a few of the Chinese paid any attention to us as we trudged on weak legs through the cold. The march was only four or five miles, but it was bad in our thin clothes after twelve days of kennel-living and starvation rations in the prison ship. Gunner McKinstry's shoes were too big for him and he was barely able to hobble on his blistered feet when we reached our destination, Woosung prison camp.

Another American prisoner had been brought aboard before we dropped downriver from Shanghai to Woosung. He was Lieutenant Commander Columbus Smith, Commanding Officer of the gunboat *Wake*, which had been seized at Shanghai when the war started.

Somebody said, "The *Wake*, eh? What do you think of the name?"

"I guess it's just unlucky," Commander Cunningham said.

Chapter Fifteen

Prison Camp

THERE MAY BE MORE BLEAK and desolate places on this earth than Woosung prison camp, but I have never seen them. The prisoners' quarters were seven ramshackle barracks—each a long, narrow, one-story shanty into which the Japs crowded two hundred men. At one end of each barracks was a wash rack and toilets. Facing the toilets, and much too close for sanitation, was a galley where food was prepared. The only other buildings on the barren wasteland of the camp area were administrative offices, guards' quarters and storerooms. The camp was surrounded by an electrified fence; and later, inside that fence, another electrified fence was erected around the barracks and the toilets.

The prisoners slept on wooden platforms and each man was given a straw tick and four blankets for his bedding, but four of those skimpy blankets were not half as warm as one ordinary American blanket. The jerry-built barracks gave little protection against the intense cold, and during the bitter winter we were soon pooling our blankets and sleeping four in a bunk to keep from freezing to death. The North China Marines who joined us at Woosung had winter uniforms, with overcoats, fur hats and gloves, but the rest of us had only the thin tropical uniforms we had brought from Wake. During the whole time of our captivity, the cold was our bitterest hardship and our suffering was made worse because we never had enough to eat.

Rice and "tea" were standard for all meals. The "tea" was made from willow leaves and the rice was often so full of pebbles that prisoners broke their teeth trying to eat it. We also frequently had a weird stew, usually too thin for nourishment. When it was even thinner than usual, the sardonic Marines called it "Tojo water." In addition, the Red Cross sent supplies every two weeks after the summer of 1942, and we also had what vegetables we could raise in our garden.

The guards were brutal, stupid, or both. They seemed to delight in every form of abuse, from petty harrassment to sadistic torture, and if the camp authorities did not actually foster this cruelty, they did nothing to stop it.

Of all the Japs who had a crack at us in the six prison camps in which I was held during our captivity, the most insatiably brutal was Ishihara, a civilian interpreter. He had learned English in Honolulu, where he had gone to school and later worked as a truck driver. He was about thirty-five, slightly built and wore horn-rimmed spectacles. The men he flogged, kicked and abused tagged him the "Beast of the East."

One of Ishihara's first victims at Woosung was Second Lieutenant Huisenga, a former football star at Annapolis. Huisenga, a North China Marine, had borrowed some tools from our own carpenter to make a few repairs in his quarters. Ishihara heard of it and snatched up a club. He rushed at Huisenga in a frenzy, clubbing him down, pounding him in wild fury until the helpless prisoner was unconscious. Then the panting Ishihara looked around him, smirking in triumph, safe under the rifles of the guards.

Sir Mark Young, the British Governor General of Hong Kong, also did something or other that angered Ishihara, possibly no more than failing to show properly servile respect for a Japanese civilian interpreter.

This time Ishihara whipped out a sword, swinging it back to strike Sir Mark, but a Marine jumped him. Major Luther A. Brown, commander of the Marine Barracks at Tientsin, twisted the sword out of Ishihara's hand and made the raging Jap back down.

For once, the Jap officials did not back up a brutal underling. Colonel Yuse, the camp commandant, forbade Ishihara to carry a sword, probably more because Ishihara was a civilian than because of any desire to protect us. After that, Ishihara had to do his slashing of prisoners with a riding crop.

When Colonel Yuse died in the fall of '42, he was succeeded as camp commandant by Colonel Otera, whom the Marines dubbed "Handle-bar Hank" because of his majestic moustache. He was a chronic drunk, and we heard that his love of the bottle was the reason Handle-bar Hank was only a colonel while many of his classmates at the Officers' School were major generals and lieutenant generals. He didn't seem to mind, though; in fact, he didn't seem to mind anything so long as he could stay mellow. He didn't pay much attention to the prisoners or anything else in the camp, and his chauffeur became our best source of contraband, especially electric hot plates, which were strictly forbidden in the prisoners' barracks.

Then there was "Tiny Tim," a rambunctious officer whose favorite recreation was running us through surprise drills and inspections. Prisoners who had worked like slaves all day would be broken out at weird hours for fire drill or inspection, and there didn't seem to be anything we could do about it. But he finally sprung one fire drill too many, and one of the fire extinguishers "happened" to get out of control just as Tiny Tim was strutting past in his best uniform. He lost interest in surprise drills after that.

Colonel William W. Ashurst, of the North China Marines, as senior officer present, continually protested against infringements of international law in the treatment of the prisoners, but there was little else we could do to stop the petty persecution or even senseless cruelty of the Japanese guards. The prisoners could only take it in silence and store up hate in their hearts. The Japanese attitude toward us was, I think, most succinctly expressed in a Christmas address to prisoners by one Jap commander:

"From now on, you have no property. You gave up everything when you surrendered. You do not even own the air that is in your bodies. From now on, you will work for the building of Greater Asia. You are the slaves of the Japanese."

That is why "Popeye" stands out like a bright light in the memory of that black time. He was one of our guards, a young Formosan who had been a hotel clerk in civil life. He treated the prisoners like human beings. He secretly gave us cigarettes and even money to buy smuggled necessities, and he refused to accept anything in return. He was simply a decent man, which made him unique among the Jap guards we encountered. I hope Popeye came through the war and I hope he fares well wherever he is. He rates it.

The camp routine varied with the season, of course, but the chief difference was merely that in summer we got up earlier and stayed up later. Our day usually began at 5:30 a.m. Immediately after the bugler sounded the discordant din of Japanese reveille, we were mustered in the barracks for roll call and inspection. Bunks had to be neat, blankets folded and shoes "washed." We tried for months to explain to camp officials what a daily washing did to leather shoes but they only shrugged. The order said that prisoners' shoes should be "washed" for inspection, and that was the way it would be as long as our shoes lasted.

I was adjutant in charge of my barracks, and as the inspecting party arrived I would sing out, *"Ki wo tsuki!"* (Attention!) Then, *"Bango!"* (Count off!), and the men would shout:

"Ichi!"
"Ni!"
"San!"
"Shi!"

When the inspecting party had left, I would order, "Yasume!" (Rest!), which was about the extent of our fluency in Japanese despite an attempt by the camp director to make us learn the language. He formed classes for the American officers, with compulsory attendance, but the classes met only twice. As was so often the case, the Japs started enterprises with elaborate plans and then lost interest. I was reminded of Kipling's Bandar-log.

After inspection, we had breakfast and then the working parties of prisoners were formed, some being taken by trucks to labor on roads and other jobs outside of camp, while the rest worked in the camp garden, policed the grounds and buildings or washed their clothes.

We had a dab of midday lunch, then more hours of work until supper was dished out about 6:00 p.m. or whenever the outside working parties returned. Evening roll call was at 8:30 p.m. and taps sounded between 9:00 p.m. and 11:00 p.m. depending on the season. Lights went out at taps. Then the hungry, weary prisoners lay in the dark, trying to forget the thoughts a man can't forget, hoping to sleep until the bugle called them out to slave again.

That was our routine, our way of life for almost four years—except when it was worse. But all that is only part of the story of our captivity, the easiest part. Hidden behind the routine, under the surface of life in prison camp, was fought a war of wills for moral supremacy—an endless struggle, as bitter as it was unspoken, between the captors and the captives. The stake seemed to me simply this: the main objective of the whole Japanese prison program was to break our spirit, and on our side was a stubborn determination to keep our self-respect whatever else they took from us. It seems to me that struggle was almost as much a part of the war as the battle we fought on Wake Island. This is how it went.

At Woosung, the main task of the prisoners was road repair, but the Americans were so conscientiously slipshod in their work and so adept at the slowdown that the Japs finally gave up. They assigned the prisoners to make a big camp garden instead, but after the seeds were planted, there was not enough work to keep the men busy. There was nothing for them to do but loaf around, and we knew there was danger in that. Idleness in prison will break a man. So we tried to patch together a program of activities to keep the men occupied, though there wasn't much we could do with our limited facilities. I obtained permission from the Jap commander to start a school with American officers as teachers. We attempted to teach only high school subjects and attendance was not compulsory, but men came. I don't know how much they learned, but it helped to pass the bleak days and keep our minds off our troubles. We laid out a baseball diamond; and some of the men took up whittling or built model planes, though we had only makeshift tools and materials for such handicraft. The camp's champion whittler was an old Army man, a master sergeant, whose specialty was fancy cigarette holders. Such was our shortage of consumer goods that he sold all he could make.

The Japanese, master of life and death, overlooked no chance, however petty, to strike at our pride, to try to make us lose face. Typical was the order that we must salute Jap non-coms as we did their officers. We found a way out of that: we simply failed to obey except when a Jap non-com was officer of the day, which was in accord with accepted military custom. I have heard of cases where the Japanese executed prisoners for less than that, but for some reason the Jap at Woosung did not press the point.

We were short of everything, of course—food and clothing and everything else—but we would have been far worse off had it not been for the American and British residents of Shanghai. They sent us books and whatever else they could spare. I remember especially Mrs. Percy Shelley Widdup, whom we came to know as "Aunt Bee." She informally adopted fourteen of the Wake Island officers and sent us food and knitted-wear that was worth more than any money when winter came. The Japs made a great fuss about the number of gifts she sent, but they finally let her parcels pass after she explained that all fourteen of us were her "nephews."

When our first Red Cross boxes arrived at Christmas, 1942, a year after our capture, we found the Japs had looted them. Red Cross food was even seen on the camp commandant's shelves. Colonel Ashurst finally stopped such thefts by refusing to sign for the boxes as senior officer unless the prisoners got them intact. Altogether, each of us received seventeen and one-half Red Cross boxes, and it is only stating a simple fact to say that these boxes saved our lives. The food and the medical supplies we got from home and from our friends in Shanghai enabled our prisoner doctors to keep our death rate during that time about what it would have been in an ordinary community.

The food saved us, yes; but as bad as our hunger for food was the hunger for news from home. Not knowing is almost as bad as anything you have to face in prison camp. A man begins to wonder, beating his brains, dreaming up dark things and brooding on them, wondering and worrying, and finally he's licked. That is when he loses the battle to keep his pride.

The Japanese refused to let us write home until more than six months after we had been taken prisoner. We did not get our first mail from home until the fall of 1942, almost a year after the surrender. In all, we got mail from home only about a dozen times. Sometimes the Japanese censored our letters by cutting out passages. Sometimes they confiscated the entire letter without letting the prisoner know that somebody had written to him.

The Japs also made a practice of holding up our mail after it had arrived. I know that one big batch of mail arrived for us in November, 1943, and the Japs delayed giving all of it to us until March, 1944. That may seem a petty persecution, but to men in prison camp it was torture. Men who were brave in battle have cried in the dark because they didn't get a letter. Exhausted men have lain all night staring at the raw ceiling, trying to stop wondering what's happening at home. It's just one last thing on top of all the rest.

We had one strong weapon to use against the breaking of pride. That is why we insisted from the start on maintaining military discipline among the prisoners. It was the only way we could continue as a military organization and not become a mob. It was only by maintaining the officers status that we could properly represent our men in dealing with the Japs and get things for them from our captors. And it was only by maintenance of discipline as a military organization that we were able to keep our morale through the years of our captivity.

My insistence on saluting in prison camp may seem absurd to some, but I know that in prison camp, when the military personnel exchanged salutes, it made us feel that, despite our ragged clothes and empty bellies, we were still a part of something the Japs couldn't break. It helped us keep our pride, our self-respect, our sense of maintaining a code in the face of disaster. In spite of everything we still belonged.

A serious problem in prison camp, as in any place where men live in such close proximity, was created by conflict of personalities and ideas among ourselves. Of course, more often than not, these disagreements turned molehills into mountains because of the conditions of our life, but here again the maintenance of discipline solved our problem and kept us united in our opposition to the Japs' attempts to break us.

Every time a draft of prisoners was taken away, I gave each man an identification paper. It was just a slip typed out by the clerk, saying that Pfc So-and-So was a member of the Wake Island Detachment of the First Marine Defense Battalion. In my presence, the man signed his identification paper and I certified it by my signature. It didn't mean much, of course—probably nothing in itself—but I felt it was a straw of group identity to which a man could cling no matter where he went. It was something to remind him he was an American and a Marine, still part of something and not alone, whatever the Japs did to him. There are men who still treasure those scraps of paper.

None of us ever doubted that America would win the war, but sometimes a man might wonder whether he would be alive to see the end. We knew so little at first of what was happening beyond the electric fence that was the boundary of our world. Old newspapers reached us once in a while and each one passed from hand to hand until it was shredded. The Japs also allowed us to have a radio in each barracks, but the radios were set so we could receive only from the French, German and Russian stations in Shanghai which made English broadcasts. Soon, however, we were secretly receiving broadcasts from the States. I don't know how it was done and I never asked. You learn not to ask questions about a thing like that in prison camp. All I know is that Lieutenant Kinney took our barracks radio and tinkered with it and after that he was able to tell us the day's news from the States. There was not much to make us cheerful in the news that spring of 1942 except for Doolittle's raid, but then came that wonderful day when Kinney told us about the Battle of the Coral Sea.

I mentioned that the Japanese allowed us to write our

first letters home in the summer of 1942. I wrote to my wife and my son Paddy. The International Red Cross notified my wife in June that I was alive, but before my letter reached her she had died. It was August before I learned of her death from the Red Cross.

The Japanese officials expressed their sympathy and told me I could knock off work for three days if I had "the proper attitude"—whatever that meant. I believe they were trying to do the right thing, but as usual they succeeded only in being clumsy and intrusive.

It was April, 1943, almost a year after my wife's death, before I was allowed to write to Paddy. He was nine and was living with my wife's parents, Colonel and Mrs. J.P. Welch, at the Army post on Governor's Island. I print this letter here because it was part of my life in prison camp and because it is a compromised document. Having been given to the press at the time, it no longer has the character of privacy intended when I wrote it.

Dear Paddy:

Our loss must have indeed been a shock to you; it was to me. We both loved her so much. I only wish that I could be with you, but you are indeed fortunate to have your grandparents to watch over you. I made a broadcast recording to you last fall. Do hope you received it in view of the fact that this is my first letter to you. Impossible to write more often.

In your mother's letter she said you were doing well in church and school. Keep up the good work. You will find both extremely necessary in later life. Since I can't do it, will you please ask your grandmother to have you given swimming and riding lessons. I do not care how well you are able to perform when I return, but I do want you to like riding. You will have to help me school horses when we get our farm. Speaking of farming, I am learning quite a bit about it. We have textbooks and practical experience plus lots of advice.

Your mother wrote you were "throwing your weight around" the post on account of the Wake Island Marines. They did quite well and I am proud of them, but remember that it just so happened we were there. Anyone else would have done the same. You must remember that the work done behind the lines is often more vital than that at the front.

You can see from the enclosed picture which was taken this winter that I am well as are most of us. Of course we would like to be going home and if an exchange is made, we should be among the first.

Please write as often as possible. My only letters were dated last June. I suppose you were able to be with your cousins for a while last summer and imagine that you will get to Chevy Chase this coming summer. As I have written before, I would like you to visit any of your cousins whenever it is possible.

Be sure and write everyone saying you have heard from me and give them my love.

Your affectionate father,
Daddy.

Chapter Sixteen

"The Mount Fuji Project"

IN DECEMBER, 1942, AFTER A guerilla sniper shot a Jap sentry at Woosung, we were marched to another prison camp five miles away at Kiang Wang. The camp was almost a duplicate of Woosung, but the Marines remember Kiang Wang as the worst hellhole of our captivity because of the "Mount Fuji project." That was the Marines' name for a construction job on which they were forced to slave twelve hours a day, six days a week, under Ishihara's sadistic supervision. The project was ostensibly a recreation park but actually a rifle range, and Ishihara drove the prisoners so brutally that weakened men began to drop, unable to stand the merciless pace. Ishihara only drove the others harder.

Most of the prisoners had no money except what they were paid for working. The pay varied according to rank, with officers getting more than enlisted personnel. As Chinese money was practically worthless, a private had to work three days to earn the price of ten cigarettes or a small loaf of Jap bread.

Some of the prisoners, especially the North China Marines, were more fortunate. They had been able to bring in American currency with which they could buy Chinese money or military yen in which all purchases had to be made, but the official rate was so low that they refused to part with their American dollars and snooped around for a black market. They found one through the Chinese coolies at Mount Fuji. Ishihara got his cut for winking at this black market dealing, but he was so greedy that he kept insisting on more and more until the men shut down on him. Then he squealed to the camp officials and demanded an investigation to stamp out the iniquitous practice.

That was the beginning of the worst inquisition of our captivity. Lieutenant (jg) Foley, a Navy medical officer from Tientsin, was one of the first called for questioning. After the "questioning" he was carried out on a stretcher, unconscious. Suspected prisoners—officers and men—were called to the torture. They were beaten until they could not stand. Men's thumbs were twisted until it seemed they were being torn off. Some were given "the water cure"—a tube was jabbed into their mouths and water was poured down it until they fainted. Not one of them admitted anything.

Colonel Ashurst and I were among the few officers who escaped interrogation. His seniority spared him, but the only reason I have ever been able to guess for my own escape was the fact that I speak a little French. Colonel Otera, the drunken camp commandant, also spoke a little and he liked to exchange a few words of French with me during his inspections. I think the sight of us chatting together in French convinced the dumb guards that I was somehow under his special protection and so they skipped me.

The Japs finally pieced together the story of the Mount Fuji black market—or part of it—from the confessions of Chinese go-betweens and information given by a "white mouse" among our civilian prisoners. The prisoners they named as guilty were put in the brig overnight and confined to baracks for a month. The white mouse's reward for squealing was promotion to *honcho,* or straw boss, but none of the other prisoners ever spoke to him again.

By the summer of 1943, the Mount Fuji project was

breaking the men's health. Tuberculosis spread and even those men still on their feet were hardly more than skin and bones. I remember one prisoner whose waistline shrank eight inches under the Japanese system of reducing. Commander Leo Thyson, (MC) USN, our senior medical officer, segregated the tuberculosis patients and insisted that they have complete rest, but that was all we could do for them. We were never able to obtain medical instruments so that our doctors could collapse the diseased lungs, though these instruments were available in the cosmopolitan city of Shanghai.

When the Mount Fuji project was finished—a blessed day for the prisoners—some of them were assigned to work at a gasoline-and-alcohol dump where they combined sabotage with pleasure by tapping the Japs' alcohol supply, for beverage purposes. The problem of getting the purloined alcohol from the dump to the prisoner's barracks was solved by a Marine who stole a section of inner tube from the tire repair shop. He sealed one end of the tube, filled it with alcohol, sealed the other end, and then wore it like a girdle as he passed empty-handed and unsuspected past the watchful guards.

As we officers had feared, the men were not in physical shape to handle alcohol and it wasn't long before a Marine was caught drunk. When he was sober enough to talk, the Japs insisted that he tell them why he had stolen the alcohol.

"It's like this," he said. "I've got aches in my bones and I need it for massage."

The Japs not only swallowed the tale, but let him take along a bottle of alcohol "for massage" while he was in the brig, which made him the most envied man in camp, brig or no brig.

Only a week or so after his release from the brig, this Marine was again found intoxicated. A second offense was such a serious matter that he was hauled up before Colonel Otera himself. And what, demanded the outraged colonel, should be done with such a habitual offender?

The Marine replied, "I don't know, sir. I reckon you better shoot me."

Colonel Otera was so flabbergasted that he let the prisoner off with a warning.

During the whole period of our captivity, I suppose the most constant thought in the mind of any prisoner was his chances of escape. The first attempt after our arrival at Woosung was made by five prisoners in March, 1942. Two of the five were from Wake Island: Commander Cunningham and Mr. Teters. They crawled under the electrified fence and struck out afoot across country in the hope of finding one of the Chinese guerilla bands, but they were caught within twenty-four hours and brought back to Woosung. The five prisoners were paraded as a warning to the rest of us before being taken to Shanghai for trial. The military personnel were sentenced to ten years' close confinement in prison for the crime of "desertion from the Japanese Army."

Commander Cunningham took the risk of attempting to escape because he had information which he considered of great importance to our Navy, but I had no such incentive. Quartermaster Clerk Paul Chandler subsequently took back to Washington the only contribution I could make to our military intelligence.

Chandler had been taken prisoner in Shanghai. He was a Marine, but he had diplomatic status because he was attached to the consular service to complete negotiations for property sales after the Fourth Marines had been evacuated from Shanghai before the outbreak of war. Some time after the Shanghai prisoners joined us, the word went around that prisoners with diplomatic status and some civilians would soon be repatriated. So I had a little private talk with Chandler. I gave him our casualty figures and a list of our dead and told him to inform Headquarters. I also told him to report orally how the Japanese had succeeded in their final attack—by landing at night and without naval gunfire support. A little later, the prisoners to be repatriated were put under close guard. I suppose it was to prevent us sending messages, but again the Japs were a little too late.

Consequently, I did not consider myself justified in making an attempt to escape since I was one of the senior Marine officers. I considered it my duty to stay with my men as long as I could, to maintain discipline and morale, to represent them to the Japanese authorities and to keep as many of them as I could alive until the war was over. I realize my decision was hardly in the adventure-yarn tradition, but I feel that events justified it. Anyway, nobody ever made good an escape from Woosung or Kiang Wang.

In 1943, there was a shortage of labor in Japan and a group from our camp was transported to Osaka. Corporal Gross was one of those to go. "We feared this," he said, "as we could have been sunk by one of our own submarines. But our group arrived in Camp Tsumori, near the shipyards, and we ended up working like slaves. We got a bowl of rice twice a day that could have been put in a teacup. At noon we got three little pieces of bread and, once in a while, about every two weeks, our captors would boil fish in with the rice to make a watery soup. It had no salt, but sometimes would have sweet potato and carrot tops in it that usually are discarded."

We were now able to follow the progress of the war fairly well through radios surreptitiously constructed of odds and ends and baling wire and from news brought to camp by fresh drafts of prisoners. We were elated but not greatly surprised when B-29's began to bomb Jap installations around Shanghai in the winter of 1944. Our big thrill came in the spring of 1945 when a flight of P-51's passed over us so low that we waved to the pilots. Army fighter planes meant that Americans had established a base not too far away. For the first time in three years, I heard Marines whistling as they worked.

The more the American planes struck, the more hysterical our guards became. When the air raid warning sounded, they would herd us into the barracks, jabbing with their bayonets and screaming at us. Once they lost their heads so completely that they fired at raiding planes from the windows of our barracks. This was a violation of the rules of war, but their terrified, ineffectual fire did more to amuse us than to arouse our indignation.

Early in May, leaving behind about two dozen tuberculars and mental cases, the Japs began moving us seven hundred miles northward to Fengtai, near Peking. They loaded us into freight cars for the trip. The officers were lucky: only twenty-five of us were put in each car, while enlisted men and civilians were crammed in fifty to the car, none of which was big enough to allow fifty men to lie down at the same time.

The middle section of each car between the sliding doors was wired off to keep the prisoners in the end sections from rushing the guards. Each car had four small windows, also covered with wire. At night, each car was lit by a single oil lamp. Men soon noticed that if clothing were hung in a certain way near the lamp, one window at a time could be screened from the light. Then they noticed that the wires across the windows were loose, the guards were drowsing and the train was making barely twenty miles an hour.

The next night the train jerked suddenly to a stop. Enraged Jap officers clambered in with drawn pistols and swords, squealing in rage as they counted heads and spouted threats. We learned later that five officers had escaped through the window of the car ahead: Lieutenants Kinney and McAlister, of the Wake Islanders; Huizenga and McBrayer, of the North China Marines; and Bishop, a Flying Tiger.

Colonel Otera was so outraged that he announced he

was placing himself under arrest. Elaborate precautions were taken to prevent any further escapes, the windows were wedged and an officer with a drawn sword took his post in the guard's section of each car, but the next night two civilian prisoners escaped. One of the civilians was recaptured and so viciously abused that he suffered a breakdown, but the other civilian and the five officers made their way safely across country to friendly troops.

The escaped prisoners separated as they fled from the train, but were reunited after reaching guerila bands of Chinese Communists. During the next forty-seven days, they traveled about seven hundred miles by foot, horse and boat through and around Japanese territory. In a report made after his return to the States, Lieutenant McAlister said that with the Chinese Communists they traveled thirty-three days in enemy territory "hitherto without U.S. or Kuomintang observers. In this area of the Chinese Communists our treatment was excellent. The Communists gave us food, medicine, clothing and $100,000 in Chinese currency. We visited most of their factories, schools, hospitals and army and guerila units." The Americans were passed on to Nationalist troops and, "for a period of fourteen days while in Kuomintang territory, we were accorded excellent treatment by Nationalist Government troops behind the enemy lines. Here again we attended war rallies and visited Army units along our path."

It took our train five days to reach Fengtai, where we found fewer facilities and worse food than at Woosung or Kiang Wang. On June 19, we began another boxcar trip, this time of four days to the port of Fusan in Korea. We arrived in a cloudburst and had to march three miles through ankle-deep mud to camp. Some of the prisoners were elderly, all were weak, but the Japs kept prodding us on, refusing to let us try to help men who slipped and fell in the mud. I still can't forget a one-legged pilot trying to hobble through the mud on crude crutches we had made for him.

Fusan was worse than Fengtai. We had to brush away swarms of flies with one hand while we tried to eat with the other. The food was like garbage. Almost all of us had dysentery. The third day after our arrival, they marched us to the docks and packed us into the fetid, airless lower deck of a ferry steamer. The twelve hour passage to Honshu, Japan's main island, was worse than our nine days in the boxcars. Then we were loaded into day coaches, 170 prisoners jammed into a car built to hold 88. The guards made us keep the blinds drawn, but we managed to steal glimpses of the country through which we were passing. For miles along both sides of the tracks there was nothing left except rubble and ruin. Weak and worn as we were, the sight made us grin at each other.

We knew only that we were going north. We got a change of rations. Instead of raw fish with our rice, the guards gave us cooked food—fried grasshoppers. By train and ferry, we finally reached Takagawa, on Hokkaido, July 6. There thirty-five of us officers were separated from the men. We were being taken to another camp. I barely had time to remind the men that they must stick together, that they must maintain discipline as Marines, when we were taken on to Nishiashibetsu, some twenty miles from Takagawa. We found forty-five Australian officers already there. They had been captured at Rabaul and were only shambling skeletons after their years of captivity in the prison camp at Zentsuji. When the Japs made us "volunteer" for manual labor, the Australians were the first to agree because it meant they would be given an extra ration of rice.

We were put to work clearing ground for a garden, but within a month most of the officers were transferred to a lumberyard and set to carrying timbers and gravel to a nearby coal mine. Enlisted men from the camps around us were forced to work underground at the mines in shifts of twelve and fourteen hours a day.

We did not hear about the atomic bomb.

One day Lieutenant Commander Greey and I passed some British Tommies as we came back from work. One of the Tommies said, "We've having a bowl of caviar tonight." We were told another Tommy had muttered to an officer, "Sir, Joe is in." That was how we learned that Russia had declared war on Japan.

The guards began singing a softer tune. They even allowed us to swim in the river below camp. There a Jap soldier confided to us in schoolboy English, "Very soon we will all be friends again."

The Japs had a radio in their office in our barracks, but we never knew what the announcer was saying. One day the Japs began crowding into the office. There were even women pressing in to hear the radio.

A prisoner said, "They're gathering all their people for it. It must be something big."

We sat listening to the blaring radio, wondering what the announcer was jabbering, and then we heard a woman scream. She worked in their galley. Now she was screaming and sobbing at what she had heard. As they left, all the Japs looked sick.

One of us said, "Something sure as hell has happened."

That was August 14. The Japs had just heard the announcement of Japan's surrender. But nobody told us about it. All they did was announce that next day there would be no working parties.

Then it seemed that every day was Christmas. Our cigarette ration had started at ten a day at Woosung and had shrunk to nothing. Now the cigarette ration was restored. We started getting some decent food, vegetables and even sugar. The guards became steadily more friendly. We knew the war had taken a big change, but we got the impression it was only some sort of armistice because the Japs didn't relinquish control; they only relaxed their strictness little by little. The captive officers still went on wood-gathering details, still cooked their own food, still policed their heads (latrines).

Then on August 18, an English-speaking Jap officer announced to the prisoners, "We have decided to stop fighting though our Army has not been beaten in the field."

Some of us were allowed to go to a house nearby where a Jap translated Japanese newspapers for us, but even then we did not know Japan had surrendered unconditionally. The translator told us the Japs would keep their homeland and that the Emperor would remain in power. He gave us the idea that it was a negotiated peace, and we didn't learn the truth until August 20 when the International Red Cross representatives arrived at our camp.

Before the Red Cross men arrived, the Japs rigged up a "first aid room" in our barracks, fitting it with medical equipment none of us had ever seen before and blandly pretended that it had been there all the time for the benefit of the prisoners.

We were burning to start home, but the word was passed that we would remain in the camps until records could be checked and transportation arranged. We had been taking over the camp administration little by little and about September 5, I went over to one of the men's camps—most of the prisoners there were my men—and took command. Among the first of my men I saw was my former orderly, Pfc H.D. (Rocky) Lorenz, who had taken such excellent care of me during our long imprisonment, doing what he could for me when not forced to work for the Japanese.

One night the Japanese gave a dinner party for us at the mine officials' club. We went because we felt that perhaps it would reassure the Jap people that we were not the ruthless barbarians their propagandists had insisted throughout the war. Possibly that might help a little in peaceful occupation of the country, if that were a condition of the surrender. Our incomplete information still lead us to believe that only a few strategic points would be taken over.

Our Japanese hosts were generous with good food and wine, but then the top official had the gall to propose a toast to "everlasting friendship between America and Japan." Major Brown, of the North China Marines, responded. He stood silent a moment, looking at them, remembering Ishihara, remembering the starvation and torture of our men, remembering the arrogant brutality of these people who were now fawning on us. He told them:

"If you behave yourselves, you'll get fair treatment."

A couple of American rescue teams arrived about September 10 and seemed a little disappointed that we were getting along so well. We had a radio receiver in operation and the first of our men were being started home. As instructed, I sent first the sick, the British and American merchant marine officers and some service personnel under Gunner McKinstry. The remainder were scheduled to leave September 14.

In response to a message from Rear Admiral "Beauty" Martin, I went to Chitosi airfield and took off in a Navy plane September 15. When I stepped out of that plane on the deck of Admiral Martin's flagship, the escort carrier *Hoggatt Bay,* I felt American "soil" under my feet for the first time since our surrender. There I was met by an old friend, Captain Joe Briggs, and then I dined as Admiral Martin's guest. The Admiral is a fine host—but for my first American meal he served me rice.

Admiral "Fighting Jack" Fletcher, commanding the North Pacific Fleet, put me up overnight on his flagship and then I picked up some Wake Island officers in Tokyo and took off for home. We were at Guam September 17, Pearl Harbor September 19 and Washington September 26. That is bluntly factual, but I do not think any man who was a prisoner of the Japanese will ever be able to put down in words what he felt on coming home. One thing I could not get over was the way we were treated by everybody, even by people we had never met. I think it was summed up for all of us by Colonel Samuel Howard, who commanded the Fourth Marines on Bataan and Corregidor, when he said:

"If this keeps up, they'll kill us with kindness."

But for me, the high point was a single moment when I reached Washington. There was a crowd—kinsmen, old friends and a lot of others—but in that moment the only person I saw was my son Paddy coming toward me.

Chapter Seventeen

Ambrose C. Lum

THE STORY OF WAKE ISLAND would be incomplete without special reference to a very special man, the late Ambrose C. Lum, "Honorary Pfc, United States Marines."

Ambrose was of Chinese descent, but as a native of Honolulu he was an American citizen, a fact he proudly announced when he appeared at my CP to make himself useful as an orderly and handyman when the war began. Ambrose adopted the Marines as his own, especially Corporal Robert McC. Brown, and I heard him call their attention to the fact that his feet were larger than those of the average Chinese. He explained that his feet were larger because, as an American citizen, he always had plenty of good milk, butter and eggs.

Ambrose didn't like bombs any better than the rest of us, but he didn't bother to hide his feeling. He was a quick man into a hole when the bombers came. One day as we ducked for shelter, Ambrose noticed that Corporal Brown was missing.

"Where's Bob?" he cried. "Where's Bob?"

Somebody mentioned that Corporal Brown had slipped off into the brush for a little nap. Ambrose burst out, "He'll be killed!" A moment later, despite his fear of bombs, Ambrose was streaking out into the brush to find his friend. He awoke the sleeping corporal as the first bombs came whistling down. They had only seconds to spare as they sprinted for cover. After the raid, they returned to the spot to get Corporal Brown's gear. They found a bomb crater where Brown had left his blankets.

Ambrose went to prison camp with us and there, as a Chinese, he became an invaluable contact with the black market from which he smuggled necessities and such small luxuries as we could afford. He could have gouged the American prisoners for his own profit, but he never did.

When the Japanese started their inquisition into the black market, Ambrose was promised immunity if he would turn up the Marines involved. He insisted he knew nothing. They beat him until he was unconscious, and they gave him the water cure, forcing water down his gagging throat until he fainted, but they never got a word out of him.

Then they tried kindness, trying to persuade him that he was an Asiatic; that we were his enemies; that he would benefit in privileges if he put the finger on the "guilty" Americans. All they got out of him, even when they flogged him again, was a defiant:

"I may be a yellow man like you, but I'm an American citizen! You better be careful what you do to me!"

The Japs finally gave Ambrose up as a bad job. It was for this more than for his endless wangling for our benefit that some of the Marines decided to show their gratitude in the only way they could. They "elected" him an Honorary Pfc in the United States Marine Corps. They tell me that there were tears in Ambrose's eyes when he was informed of it.

After that, Ambrose got his great idea. He had been in the canary bird business before he went to Wake and he had a lot of money safe in the bank in Honolulu. When he got home, he said, he would open a new business. It would be the most exclusive bar in the world. The name would be "THE WAKE ISLAND MARINE BAR." The only customers who would ever be admitted would be Marines or the guests of Marines. As "Honorary Pfc" Lum explained to Corporal Brown in prison camp:

"I want to show I feel the honor. Anyhow, Marines got to stick together."

I had hoped to sit down and join Ambrose in a drink when I visited the Islands. Unfortunately, a number of years passed before I returned to Hawaii, and it was then I learned that he had passed away. I shall never forget his friendship—and his courage.

THE WHITE HOUSE

WASHINGTON

4 December, 1945.

Dear James O. King,

It gives me special pleasure to welcome you back to your native shores, and to express, on behalf of the people of the United States, the joy we feel at your deliverance from the hands of the enemy. It is a source of profound satisfaction that our efforts to accomplish your return have been successful.

You have fought valiantly and have suffered greatly. As your Commander in Chief, I take pride in your past achievements and express the thanks of a grateful Nation for your services in combat and your steadfastness while a prisoner of war.

May God grant you happiness and a successful future.

Harry Truman

Wake Islander James King, who chose to remain in the Marine Corps after repatriation, had been promoted to corporal by the time he received this presidential "welcome home."

Postscript

WHEN THE WAR ENDED in 1945, we of the Wake Island Marines had been together for about four years. A few of our number had been taken from the main body from time to time and a few had died, but the main body was still intact. We had maintained military discipline within our ranks, and in a sense we had remained a military unit. All of this came to an end as we were released from prison and restored to our own forces. We were repatriated piecemeal and, as a consequence, the unit broke up rapidly.

Our officers and men went their separate ways and scattered in all directions. A significant portion continued active duty in the Armed Forces; a number of NCOs were commissioned and served the Corps with distinction in peace, in the Korean conflict, and after. With the passage of many years, at this writing in 1978, none remain on active duty; some are deceased, others are pursuing business careers, and still others are in retirement.

Upon repatriation, those of us who were already commissioned were promoted to the rank which would have been attained had we not spent most of the war as POWs. Dates of rank on the promotion list were made retroactive to the dates at which the advanced rank should have been achieved. I am sorry to say, however, that retroactive pay was not possible. Because of a quirk in the law, Army officers who were POWs received pay retroactively from their date of rank; not so the Naval and Marine officers, who were paid only from the date they were actually sworn into the new rank.

A number of Wake defenders left the service at the end of the war. They, as well as those who left the Marines in later years, went into a variety of civilian pursuits. Some became educators, some merchants, some entered religious life, others the medical profession, some became construction workers and, a few, politicians. A sampling: Eugene Lutz, upon completion of his studies at Catholic University, was ordained a priest; George Stringfield became a Baptist minister; Eugene Ryan is an Evangelist; Eschol Davis, M.D. is a practicing psychologist; Bryghte Godbold, Guy Kelnhofer and Carl Stegmaier obtained doctorates in philosophy, with entomologist Stegmaier the author of several books in his field; James King is director of a security service in San Francisco; and Jack Skaggs has one of the largest construction companies in Oklahoma City.

Though the men of Wake Island are scattered far and wide, they have held together in spirit. An unofficial society, The Defenders of Wake Island, came into being during the 1950s. Jack Skaggs got the idea when he attended a national Ex-POW convention, and he arranged the first all-Wake Island reunion in 1961. Since then, reunions have been held in 1970, 1973, 1975, and is now an annual get-together. During our 1978 reunion, held in Oklahoma City, the citizens of Bristow, Oklahoma dedicated the first Wake Island Memorial in the United States. I believe all Defenders of Wake Island feel very honored and humbled to be remembered after so many years.

In 1974, Franklin Gross began putting out a Wake Island newsletter, *the Wig-Wag,* to keep us all up to date on who is doing what. (*Wig-Wag* was the name of the information sheet we published on Wake Island prior to and during the battle.) From his original mailing list of 150, Gross has managed to locate over 100 more of our group. But there are still over 100 survivors unaccounted for. Hopefully, some of them, or their families and friends, may read this book. The Defenders of Wake Island may be contacted by writing Franklin D. Gross, 2225 South Overton, Independence, Missouri 64052.

Finally, at one of our reunions a few years ago, several wives of the Wake Islanders came to me and thanked me for the efforts I had made through the prison camp days for their husbands' well-being and getting them safely home. I think this was as touching a tribute as I have ever received. It told me that I had done the right thing in maintaining our military organization and keeping our men under normal Marine discipline.

Appendix

*Rosters of Marine, Naval and Army Personnel
engaged in the defense of Wake Island*

I. MARINE DETACHMENT
First Defense Battalion, FMF, Wake Island
and Marine Fighting Squadron 211
of Marine Aircraft Group 21
1 December 1941—31 December 1941

Part 1: Deceased Personnel

Agar, Paul R.
Allen, Jack "V"
Beaver, Darrell L.
Bedell, Henry A.
Bertels, Alton J.
Boyle, Hugh L.
Comin, Howard D.
Commers, Joseph F.
Conderman, Robert J.
Couch, Winslow
Culp, Joseph C.
Davidson, Carl R.
De Sparr, Marshall E.
Double, John F.

Edwards, Robert P.
Elrod, Henry T.
Farrar, Herbert D.
Fleming, Manton L.
Garr, Robert F., Jr.
Gilley, Ernest N., Jr.
Gleichauf, William A.
Graves, George A.
Guthrie, Frank "A"
Haley, Gifford LaF.
Halstead, William C.
Hannum, Earl R.
Hemmelgarn, Paul F.
Himelrick, John R.

Holden, Frank J.
Houde, Severe R.
Hunt, Quince A.
Katchak, John
King, Curtis P.
Koontz, Benjamin D.
Lane, Lloyd G.
Locklin, Eugene D.
Marlow, Clovis R.
Marshall, Gordon L.
McBride, James E.
Mitwalsky, Robert W.
Nanninga, Henry D.
Phipps, Ralph E.
Pickett, Ralph H.
Pratt, Robert M.

Puckett, Ray V.
Purvis, Gordon W.
Reed, Alvey A.
Renner, Francis J.
Stevens, Robert L.
Stockton, Maurice E.
Sutton, Mack P.
Taylor, Dale K.
Tokryman, Paul
Tucker, William M.
Venable, Alexander B., Jr.
Wilsford, Clyde D.
Wiskochil, Robert I.
Wright, Johnalson E.
Zurchauer, Robert, Jr.

MARINE DETACHMENT

Part 2: Some of the following men were discharged from the Marines at the end of the war; others continued their active service. However, as of September, 1978, none remain on active duty. Also, an unknown number have died during the past 33 years.

Ackley, Edwin M.
Adams, "E" "O" S.
Adams, Richard P.
Andrews, Arthur D.
Andrews, Thomas J., Jr.
Arthur, Robert O.
Austin, Rufus B.
Baker, "S" "L"
Bamford, Roger D.
Barger, Lester L.
Barnes, Earl H.
Barninger, Clarence A., Jr.

Bartelme, Herbert E.
Bastien, James S.
Beck, William D.
Beese, Fred A.
Bendenski, Joseph B.
Benedetto, Michael A.
Benjamin, Armand E.
Bennett, Arthur K.
Bentley, Joseph M.
Berkery, James M., Jr.
Blandy, John F.

Bogdonovich, Edward M.

Boley, Kenneth C.

Borchers, Orville N.

Borne, Joseph E.

Borth, Harold C.

Boscarino, James F.

Bosher, Raymond R.

Bostick, William F.

Bourquin, Robert E., Jr.

Bowsher, Walter A., Jr.

Box, Robert S., Jr.

Boyd, Berdyne

Bragg, Lorel J.

Breckenridge, Albert H.

Brown, Buell S.

Brown, Gene E.

Brown, James R.

Brown, Kenneth LeR.

Brown, Robert L.

Brown, Robert McC.

Browning, James S.

Broyles, Earl M., Jr.

Bryan, Pershing "B"

Buchanan, Gerald E.

Buckie, William B., Jr.

Buehler, William F.

Bumgarner, Alvin A.

Burford, Philip L.

Busse, Wilbur J.

Byard, Lester C.

Byer, Lawrence M.

Bryd, Harry J.

Byrne, Herbert R.

Cain, Orville J.

Calanchini, Arthur J.

Caldwell, Richard R.

Camp, Charles H.

Carr, Gerald J.

Cemeris, John

Cessna, Harry J.

Chapman, Henry H.W.

Chew, Hoyle "E"

Christenson, Alfred B.

Chudzik, Joseph T.

Clark, Emery T.

Colby, Harold G.

Comfort, Floyd H.

Cominus, Gus J.

Condra, Charley H.

Conner, Warren D.

Connor, Dennis C.

Cook, Hal, Jr.

Cook, Jack B.

Cooley, Dlemar E.

Cooper, Clarence S., Jr.

Cooper, Paul C.

Cooper, Robert E.

Cornett, John

Couch, Claude C.

Coulson, Raymond L.

Covert, Phillip G.

Cox, Roy T.

Crouch, James A.

Cunningham, Kenneth E.

Curlee, Albert C.

Curry, Robert E.

Dale, John R.

Dana, Max J.

Davis, Eschol E.

Davis, Floyd H.

Davis, Jack E.
Dawson, Harvey L.
Deeds, Robert L.
DeLoach, Emett D.
Descamps, Clarence C.
Devereux, James P.S.
Dimento, Frank
Dodge, Bernard A.
Domingue, Alton J.
Dorman, Roger
Drake, Elmer S., Jr.
Dunham, Estille G.
Durrwachter, Henry L., Jr.
Eaton, Edward F.
Economou, Michael N.
Elliott, Norman D.
Emerick, Billie E.
Enyart, Clinton H.
Everist, Joseph L.
Fields, Marshall E.
Finley, Lloyd B.
Fish, Cyrus D.
Fitzpatrick, James A.
Fleener, Gene A.
Fortuna, Stephen
Frandsen, Andrew J.
Freuler, Herbert C.
Frey, Robert L.
Frost, Lynn W.
Gardner, Douglas D.
Gardner, Glen G.
Garrison, Everett
Gatewood, Martin A.
George, John "F"
George, Joseph E., JR.

Giddens, George G.
Gilbert, Richard C.
Godbold, Bryghte D.
Godwin, William F.
Gordon, William
Gragg, Raymon
Grant, Everard M.
Graves, Leon A.
Gray, Robert L.J.
Greeley, Robert W.
Gregouire, Sylvester
Greska, Martin A.
Gross, Franklin D.
Grubb, Glenn E.
Gruber, Walter J.
Guilbeaux, Stanley P.
Hagerty, Oliver P., Jr.
Haggard, Fred D.
Haidinger, Robert F.
Hair, Steven Y.
Hall, James W.
Hamas, John
Hamel, Fred M.
Hamilton, William J.
Hanna, Robert M.
Hannah, Clyde W.
Harper, Joel E.
Harringer, Ewald
Harrison, Charles L.
Hartung, Arvel N.
Hassig, Edwin F.
Haugen, Henry
Hearn, Jack D.
Hendrickson, Russell W.
Herron, Merle

Hicks, Albert, Jr.
Hill, Charles C.
Holewinski, Ralph J.
Holmes, Charles A.
Holt, Johnson P.
Hoskison Larence D.
Houschildt, Frank H.
Hubley, George G.
Huffman, Forest
Hughes, "A" "R" Jr.
Hundley, Robert G.
Hyder, Luther "E"
Hyzer, Morris F.
Jackson, Sammy C.
Jamerson, Joseph P.
Jenkins, Haley "B"
Johnson, George LeR.
Johnson, Harland R.
Johnson, John S., Jr.
Johnson, Phillip W.
Johnson, Ralph E.
Johnson, Solon L.
Johnson, Thomas W., Jr.
Johnston, Lillard L., Jr.
Jones, Otis T.
Joyner, Paul C.
June, Randolph M.
Kaz, Norman N.
Kelnhofer, Guy J., Jr.
Kennedy, Walter T.
Kessler, Woodrow M.
Ketner, Bernard O.
Kidd, Walter
King, James O.
King, Kirby K.
Kinney, John F.

Kirk, John T.
Klein, Arthur A.
Kleponis, Vincent
Kliewer, David D.
Kohlin, Alfred T.
Krawie, John W.
Krenistki, William
Kroptavich, James S.
Kruczek, Walter J.
Langley, Edgar N.
LaPorte, Ewing E.
Larson, William C.
Latham, Joe T.
Laursen, Norman J.
Lee, Robert E.
Lepore, Anthony
Lewis, Clifton H.
Lewis, William W.
Lillard, George E.
Lindsay, Wilford J.
Lorenz, Henry D.
Lutz, Eugene J.
Madere, Joseph A.
Malleck, Donald R.
Malone, Thomas J.
Manning, Bernard H.
Martin, Gerald J.
Martin, Virgil E.
Marvin, Kenneth L.
Mathis, Charles L.
McAlister, John A.
McAmis, Terrence T.
McAnally, Winford J.
McCage, Harvey E.
McCalla, Marvin P.
McCaulley, Wade "B"

McClanahan, Wilbur C.
McDaniel, George W.
McFall, William E.
McGee, Robert H.
McKinstry, Clarence B.
McQuilling, Robert E.
McWiggins, James C.
Melton, Kenneth L.
Mercer, Harris L.
Mergenthaler, John J.
Mettscher, Leonard G.
Milbourn, Ival D.
Miller, Hershal L.
Mitchell, James P.
Moore, John P.
Morgan, "R" "C"
Moritz, LeRoy G.
Mosley, Harvery L.
Murphy, LeRoy G.
Murphy, Robert B.
Nevenzel, Jay
Nowlin, Jesse E.
O'Connell, John J.
Oelberg, Christian, Jr.
Olenowski, Michael
Owen, Lester C.
Page, Robert E.L.
Painter, John S.
Parks, Lawrence "A"
Paszkiewicz, Andrew J.
Patterson, Billy LeR.
Paul, Archie "T"
Pearce, Herbert N.
Pearsall, John E.
Pechacek, Thomas J.

Pellegrini, Alfred F.
Percy, "R" "C"
Petrick, Edward N.
Pippi, Louis
Pistole, Erwin "D"
Platt, Wesley McC.
Poindexter, Arthur A.
Polousky, Anthony
Potter, George H., Jr.
Prochaska, Albert J.
Putnam, Paul A.
Qubre, Tony T.
Quinn, Fenton "R"
Rasor, Herman L.
Ray, Sanford K.
Raymond, Samuel W.
Reed, Clifford M.
Reed, Dick L.
Reeg, Norman M.
Reeves, Joe M.
Richardson, Bernard E.
Richey, Lewis H.
Richter, Eugene V.
Rickert, Albert P.
Rietzler, Junior H.
Robinson, George LeR.
Rogers, Charles G.
Roman, Oldrich B.
Rook, Edward B.
Rozycki, Stanley J.
Rush, Dave J.
Ryan, Eugene R.
Sado, John E.
Sanders, Clifton C.
Sanders, Jacob R.

Sapp, Charles W.
Schneider, LeRoy N.
Schulz, Glenn R.
Schulze, Carl H.
Schumacker, William T.
Shellhorn, Melvin W.
Shelton, Clifford E.
Shores, Robert
Short, Ernest E.
Shugart, Eugene W.
Shumard, Gene D.
Sickels, Percy H.
Sieger, Norman P.
Silverlieb, Irving B.
Simon, Adolph
Skaggs, Jack R.
Slezak, Rudolph M.
Sloman, Wiley W.
Smith, Dempsey
Smith, Elwood M.
Smith, Gordon L.
Smith, John C.
Smith, Robert N.
Sorrell, Jesse D.
Stafford, Virgil D.
Stahl, Rudolph W., Jr.
Stegmaier, Carl E., Jr.
Stewart, Jesse L.
Stocks, Artie J.
Stowe, Joe M.
Stringfield, George W.
Sturgeon, Edward V.
Swartz, Merle E.
Switzer, Raymond C.
Tallentire, Gilson A.

Tate, Willis
Taylor, Rudolph J.
Terfansky, Joseph E.
Terry, Arthur F.
Terry, Mabry A.
Thaire, Grover E.
Tharin, Frank C.
Tipton, Wiley E.
Todd, Herman A.
Tompkins, Raymond M.
Tramposh, Charles E.
Trego, Carroll E.
Tuck, Erville R.
Tusa, Joe M.
Vardell, Virgie P.
Vaughn, James
Venable, James C.
Verga, Vincent H.
Wade, "Q" "T"
Wallace, Verne L.
Waronker, Alvin J.
Warren, Howard E.
Warsing, John W., Jr.
Webb, Henry G.
Webster, Guy P.
Weimer, Jacob G.
Wheeler, Mackie L.
Williams, Henry, Jr.
Williams, Luther
Williamson, Jack R.
Winslow, Robert E.
Woods, Chester J.
Woodward, Theodore H.
Wynne, Marion L.
Zarlenga, Joseph D.

Zellay, George P.   Zivko, Stephen M.

II. NAVAL PERSONNEL

Anderson, John B.L.
Atwood, Laurence M.
Balhorn, Marvin W.
*Barnes, James E.
Besancon, Victor C.
*Bird, Edwin A.
Brewer, Artie T.
Caldwell, Robert E.
Chambliss, Jessee R
Cook, Walter J.
Cox, James H.
Cunningham, Winfield S.
Darden, James B.
Davis, James J., Jr.
Doke, Cecil E.
*Franklin, Theodore Douglas
Fraser, Harry S.
Fuller, Andrew A.
Gerberding, Oliver L., Jr.
Greey, Elmer B.
*Gonzales, Roy J.
Henshaw, George H.
Hesson, James F.
*Hodgkins, Ray K., Jr.
Holbrooks, Benjamin
Horstman, Herbert J.
Hotchkiss, Richard L.
Howard, John R.
Johnson, Edward E.
Kahn, Gustav M.
Keene, Campbell

Kibble, Dare K.
*Kidd, Franklin B.
*Kilcoyne, Thomas P.
Krueger, Darius C.
LaFleur, Albert H.
*Lambert, John W.
Lanning, John R.
Lauff, Bernard J.
*Lechler, William R.
Lewis, George H.
Ludwich, Kirby, Jr.
Mackie, Robert J.
Manning, William H., Jr.
Mayhew, Richard C.
McCall, James F.
*McCoy, William H.
McReynolds, Wendel
Miller, Howard
Moore, Carl, Jr.
Mullen, James M., Jr.
Olcott, Chester W.
Pickering, George F.
Plate, William O.
Plecker, McPherson
Roberson, Ted "J" "D"
Robinson, James B.
Sandvold, Julian K.
Sargent, Charles A.
Skaggs, Viktor V.
Smith, Cassius E.
Thompson, Harold Ray

Thorsen, John Thomas
Tripp, Glenn Eugene
Troney, Norris Henry
Unger, John I.
Vaale, Ernest Christian
Walish, Robert C.
White, Clyde

Williams, Bermont M.
*Williams, Harold Raymond
Wilson, Franklin Marquette
Wolfe, Clarence Eugene
*Wolney, George James
Wood, Ivan S.

(This list includes those attached to the Marines)

* Deceased

III. ARMY PERSONNEL
(All Survivors)

Dilks, Carl W.
Futtrip, Paul F.
Hotchkiss, Clifford E.

Rex, James B.
Rogers, Ernest G.
Wilson, Henry Stanley

About the Author

Brigadier General James P.S. Devereux was born on February 20, 1903, in Cabana, Cuba. He was the son of an officer of the Army Medical Corps, and his father was stationed in Cuba in connection with the windup of the Spanish-American War. The family did not remain long in Cuba, or indeed in any one location, after the birth of James. He attended a number of schools in various parts of the United States as well as in foreign countries. Among them were the Army and Navy Preparatory School in Washington, D.C., and Tome School in Port Deposit, Maryland; his last school was La Villa in Lausanne, Switzerland.

In 1923, young Devereux left school and enlisted in the Marine Corps. In February, 1925, he was commissioned a second lieutenant and was assigned to duty successively in Norfolk; Philadelphia; the Marine Barracks, Quantico, Virginia; and at Guantanamo Bay, Cuba. For a short tour he was detailed to the mail guard detachment in New York, and was then ordered to the force of Marines in Nicaragua.

Upon returning to the United States in 1927, he was assigned to the *USS Utah* and subsequently was sent back to Nicaragua. Next came an assignment to duty in China where he was promoted to first lieutenant. While in China, he commanded the Mounted Detachment of the Legation Guard at Peking, the famous "Horse Marines." Throughout his life, General Devereux has maintained a special interest in horses and in mounted sports.

In 1933, following a year of duty at Quantico, he was ordered to duty as a student at the Army Coast Artillery School at Fort Monroe, Virginia. From there he was assigned back to Quantico and promoted to captain. Here he instructed in the Base Defense Weapons School and assisted in the preparation of a Marine Corps Manual on Base Defense Weapons. General Devereux was then assigned to the Fleet Machine Gun School on the *USS Utah*. During this tour he participated in experimental antiaircraft machine gun fire and in the instruction of personnel of the Pacific Fleet.

In 1938 came duty at the Marine Corps Base, San Diego, California, where the Defense Battalion concept was being developed. Here he was promoted to the rank of major. In January, 1941, he was ordered to Pearl Harbor, and later that year went to Wake Island to assume command of the Detachment of the 1st Marine Defense Battalion. He held this command when war broke out on December 7th. By his gallant conduct of the defense of Wake against the attack of an overwhelmingly superior Japanese force he won the Navy Cross. His citation reads in part: "For distinguished and heroic conduct in the line of his profession in the defense of Wake Island . . . ."

The defense of Wake added a brilliant page to the annals of Marine tradition. The defense force went down after two weeks of Japanese attack from air and sea, but in going they took a tremendous toll of enemy manpower and equipment.

General Devereux spent the rest of the war as a POW in China and Japan. When he was repatriated at the end of the war, he was ordered to Marine Corps Headquarters to give his personal account of the defense of Wake to General Alexander A. Vandegrift,

Commandant of the Marine Corps.

Later he was assigned to the Amphibious Warfare School at Quantico and then to the 1st Marine Division at Camp Pendleton, California. He had been promoted to the rank of colonel with date of rank 1942 upon repatriation. After twenty-five years of service, James P.S. Devereux retired from active duty on August 1, 1948. He was promoted to Brigadier General upon retirement.

General Devereux's long career of service to the country was not, however, at an end. He next ran for Congress and was elected for four consecutive terms of office from his native Maryland. He relinquished his seat in the House of Representatives to make an unsuccessful run for Governor of Maryland. Subsequently, he was appointed Director of Public Safety for Baltimore County.

In 1932, while still a first lieutenant, he had married Mary Welch, the daughter of an officer of the United States Army. One son, Paddy, was born of this marriage. Mrs. Devereux died while her husband was in Prisoner of War camp, and Paddy lived with his grandparents during the war. After returning home, General Devereux married Rachel Cooke, and two sons, John Pierre and Francis Irving Cooke, were born of this marriage. The second Mrs. Devereux passed away in March, 1977. General Devereux married Edna Burnside Howard, the widow of a colonel in the Maryland National Guard in July, 1978. Between them, they have twenty grandchildren.

At present, General Devereux lives in the country north of Baltimore. He maintains an active interest in military affairs, in politics and, of course, in horse activities.